Super Cheap Paris Travel Guide 2019

Don't leave Paris without seeing (at least from outside)	80
Enjoy your first Day for under $20	84
Need to Know	87
Cheapest route to Paris from America	88
Mains under 5 euros	89
Avoid these tourist traps or scams	91
Basic Phrases	92
Getting Out	93
RECAP: How to have a $1,000 trip to Paris on a $200 budget	95
Personal Cost Breakdown	97
Thank you for reading	103
Thank you for reading	104
Bonus Budget Travel Hacks	108
How to find the freedom to travel	110
HOW TO FIND CHEAP FLIGHTS	114
Frequent Flyer Memberships	118
Pack like a Pro	119
Checks to Avoid Fees	120
Relaxing at the airport	122
Money: How to make it, spend it and save it while travelling	124
How to earn money WHILE travelling	125

How to spend money	127
How to save money while travelling	130
Travel Apps That'll Make Budget Travel Easier	132
How NOT to be ripped off	133
Small tweaks on the road add up to big differences in your bank balance	136
Where and How to Make Friends	139
When unpleasantries come your way…	140
Your Car rental insurance is crazy expensive	143
The best Travel Gadgets	148
Hacks for Families	150
Safety	153
Hilarious Travel Stories	155
How I got hooked on budget travelling	158
A final word…	160
Our Writers	161
Copyright	165

Our Mission

Like Simon Sinek said, "People don't buy what you do; they buy why you do it". We believe strongly that travel can and is best enjoyed on a budget.

Taking a trip to Paris is not just an outer journey, it's an inner one. Budget travel brings us closer to locals, culture and authenticity; which in turn makes our inner journeys more peaceful.

Travelling is painted as an expensive hobby; Travel guides, Travel bloggers and influencers often show you overpriced accommodation, restaurants and big-ticket attractions because they make money from our 'we're on vacation' mentality which leads to reckless spending. Our mission is to teach you how to enjoy more for less and get the best value from every Euro you spend in Paris.

This guide focuses on the cheap or free in Paris, but there is little value in travelling to Paris and not experiencing all it has to offer. Where possible we've included cheap workarounds or listed the experience in the loved but costly section - if it is worth your time and money.

We work to dispel myths, save you tons of money, teach you the local tips and tricks and help you find experiences in Paris that will flash before your eyes when you come to take your last breath on this beautiful earth.

Who this book is for and why anyone can enjoy budget travel

I've been travelling full-time for 20 years. I don't have a job and I'm not in any debt, which prompts friends and family to ask 'How can you afford to travel?'. My response? 'My passion is finding travel bargains'. This doesn't mean I do any less or sleep in dirty hostels. Someone who spends A LOT on travel hasn't planned or wants to spend their money. I believe you can live the bougie life on a budget; that's what I've been doing for the past 20 years.

Together with thrifty locals I met along the way I have funnelled my passion for travel bargains into 300 travel guides. In this guide, we have formulated a system to pass on to you, so you too can juice everything from visiting Paris while spending the least possible money.

There is a big difference between being cheap and frugal. I like to spend money on beautiful experiences, but 20 years of travel has taught me I could have a 20 cent experience that will stir my soul more than a $100 one. Of course, there are times when the reverse is true, my point is, spending money on travel is the best investment you can make but it doesn't have to be at levels set by hotels and attractions with massive ad spends and influencers who are paid small fortunes to get you to buy into something that you could have for a fraction of the cost.

I love travelling because it forces me to be present-minded. I like to have the cold hard budget busting facts to hand (which is why we've included so many one page charts, which you can use as a quick reference), but otherwise, I want to shape my own experience - and I'm sure you do too.

We have designed these travel guides to give you a unique planning tool to experience an unforgettable trip without spending the ascribed tourist budget.

When it comes to FUN budget travel, it's all about what you know. You can have all the feels without most of the bills. A few days spent planning can save you thousands. Luckily, Super Cheap Insider Guides have done the planning for you, so you can distill the information in minutes not days, leaving you to focus on what matters: immersing yourself in the sights, sounds and smells of Paris, meeting awesome new people and most importantly, feeling relaxed and happy. My sincere hope is that our tips will bring you great joy at a fraction of the price you expected.

So, grab a cup of tea, put your feet up and relax; you're about to enter the world of enjoying Paris on the cheap. Oh and don't forget a biscuit. You need energy to plan a trip of a lifetime on a budget.

Super Cheap Paris is <u>not</u> for travellers with the following needs:

1. You require a book with detailed offline travel maps. Super Cheap Guides are best used with Google Maps - download before you travel to make the most of your time and money.
2. You would like thousands of accommodation, food and attraction recommendations; by definition, cheapest is most often singular. We only include maximum value recommendations. We purposively leave out over-priced attractions when there is no workaround.
3. You would like detailed write-ups about hotels/Airbnbs/Restaurants. We are bargain hunters first and foremost. We dedicate our time to finding the best deals, not writing flowery language about their interiors. Plus things change. If I had a pound for every time I read a Lonely Planet description only to find the place totally different, I would be a rich man. Always look at online reviews for the latest up to date information.

If you want to <u>save A LOT of money</u> while comfortably enjoying an unforgettable trip to Paris, minus the marketing, hype, scams and tourist traps read on.

Redefining Super Cheap

The value you get out of Super Cheap Paris is not based on what you paid for it; its based on what you do with it. You can only do great things with it, if you believe saving money is worth your time. Charging things to your credit card and thinking 'oh I'll pay it off when I get back' is something you won't be tempted to do if you change your beliefs now. Think about what you associate with the word cheap, because you make your beliefs and your beliefs make you.

I grew up thinking you had to spend more than you could afford to have a good time travelling. Now I've visited 190 countries I know nothing is further from the truth. Before you embark upon reading our specific tips for Paris think about your associations with the word cheap.

Here are the dictionary definitions of cheap:

1. costing very little; relatively low in price; inexpensive:
a cheap dress.
2. costing little labor or trouble:
Words are cheap.
3. charging low prices:
a very cheap store.
4. **of little account; of small value; mean; shoddy:**
cheap conduct; cheap workmanship.
5. **embarrassed; sheepish:**
He felt cheap about his mistake.
6. **stingy; miserly:**
He's too cheap to buy his own brother a cup of coffee.

Three out of six definitions have extremely negative connotations. The 'super cheap' we're talking about in this book is not shoddy, embarrassed or stingy. We donate 10% of our book profits to charity (details of the charities we support are at the end of the book) so you've already donated to charity just by buying this book - how is that stingy?

We added the super to reinforce our message. Super's dictionary definition stands for 'a super quality'. Super Cheap stands for enjoying the best on the lowest budget. Question other peoples definitions of cheap so you're not blinded to possibilities, potential, and prosperity. Here are some new associations to consider forging:

Shoddy

Cheap stuff doesn't last is an adage marketing companies have drilled into consumers. However by asking vendors the right questions cheap doesn't mean something won't last, I had a $10 backpack last for 8 years and a $100 suitcase bust on the first journey. A   out of San Francisco University found that people who spent money on experiences rather than things were happier. Memories last forever, not things, even expensive things. And as we will show you during this guide you don't need to pay to create great memories.

Embarrassed

I have friends who routinely pay more to vendors because they think their money is putting food on this person's table. Paradoxically, Cuban doctors are driving taxi's because they earn more money; it's not always a good thing for the place you're visiting to pay more and can cause unwanted distortion in their culture - Airbnb pushing out renters is an obvious example. Think carefully about whether the extra money is helping people or incentivising greed.

Stingy

Cheap can be eco-friendly. Buying thrift clothes is cheap but you also help the Earth. Many travellers are often disillusioned by the reality of traveling experience since the places on our bucketlists are overcrowded. Cheap can take you away from the crowds. You can find balance and harmony being cheap. Remember,"A journey is best measured in friends, rather than miles." – Tim Cahill. And making friends is free!

A recent survey by Credit Karma found 50% of Millennials and Gen Z get into debt travelling. **Please don't allow credit card debt to be an unwanted souvenir you take home.** As you will see from this book, there's so much you can enjoy in Paris for free and so many ways to save money! You just need to want to!

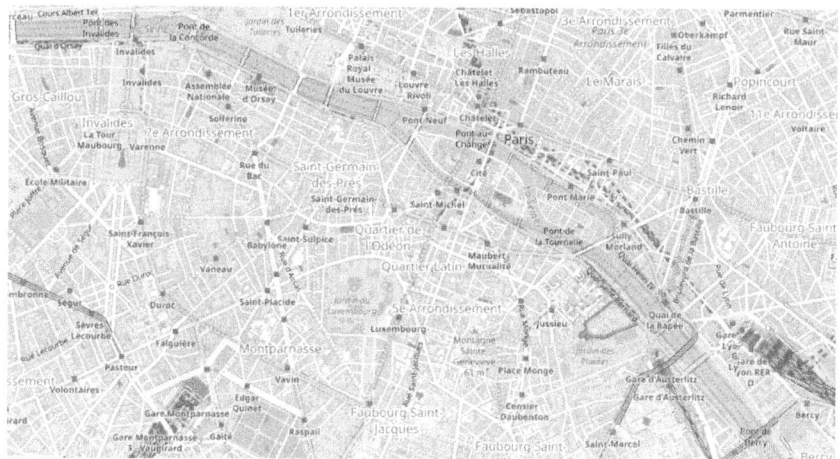

Discover Paris

Paris is everything you've imagined and more - a global trendsetter, a market leader, a thousand year old cultural capital strewn with instantly recognisable landmarks, glorious museums, cultural treasures and the best people watching.

Fashion was born in Paris; the wide boulevards gave birth to the first catwalks in the 19th century. Paris is a city of firsts: in 1915 during World War I a fraction of the Parisian army was the first to use camouflage, which comes from the French verb "to make up for the stage." The first public screening of a movie was held here in 1895. They used their invention "the cinématographe" to show 10 films of about 50 seconds each.

Paris was founded at the end of the 3rd century BC by the Gauls who were called Parisii. The Romans invaded and renamed the City "Lutetia." After almost two thousand years of tumultuous history spanning the French revolution, Napoleon and Hitler's infamous photo in front of the Eiffel tower, the modern-day city is still filled with elegant Parisians lounging outside cafés drinking coffee living its Motto: 'Liberté, Egalité, Fraternité' (Liberty, Equality, Fraternity).

Everywhere you look in Paris there is another building to photograph. There are 6,100 rues – or streets – to snap in Paris. Stroll the boulevards, shop till you drop, marvel at the Eiffel Tower (intended to stand for 20 years after being built in1889) flop riverside with a block of brie and watch the world buzz by from a streetside cafe. Savour it all.

Like any city that caters to tourists, Paris can be a budget-buster, but take heart. The trick to keeping your trip cheap but amazing is to get off the tourist track and find the local deals. If you follow the advice in this guide you could definitely get away with spending about $40 a day per person including accommodation.

Some of Paris' Best Bargains

Do a custom tour of Paris for free

Paris Greeters arranges free tours for one to six visitors with local volunteers. Submit your request online at www.greeters.paris specifying your language, interests and preferred date and time.

Get an incredible free view of the Eiffel Tower

Go to Quai Branly museum rooftop restaurant where you can sip a cheap coffee and get an incredible view of the Eiffel Tower. The Museum is free to enter.

If you're keen to visit Musée d'Orsay, go after 3pm, its cheaper and less crowded.

Take in a free performance

Visit Eglise de la Madeleine for free organ recitals, chamber concerts, and choral performances!

Visit the thrones French kings were once crowned upon for free

The Cabinet des Médailles et Monnaies on rue de Richelieu is an eclectic collection of antiques, jewellery and the 7th century Dagobert's Throne, on which French kings were once crowned. It is also the oldest museum in France and after 3pm, it's free to enter.

Eat at Michelin-starred Les Fables de la Fontaine

Lunch-menu's at Michelin-starred Les Fables de la Fontaine are shocking good value, you can indulge in a 2-course weekday lunch menu for just €28. Make reservations, the restaurant is always busy.

Le Pré Verre also has a bargainous weekday lunch menu. A starter and main (chef's choice) plus a glass of wine and coffee for just €14.90.

Indulge in Happy hours

At La Cordonnerie pints and bottles of French beer are just €3 during happy hour (5pm to 8.30pm).

Planning your trip

Go in Spring or Fall

The first step in saving money on your Paris trip is timing. If you are not tied to school holidays, the best time to visit is during the shoulder-season months of April or October, the weather is conducive to long hours of sightseeing and the summer crowds haven't yet arrived. The cheapest times to visit (prices drop 30% for accommodation then) are December, January, and February - it is cold and wet but still as beautiful.

Month-by-month

January - La Grande Parade de Montmartre. Since 1993 thousands have flocked to Paris' 18th Arrondissment for this annual colourful parade.

February - Chinese New Year Celebrations Every year a huge parade marches its way through Paris' 'Quartier Chinois' to celebrate the coming of the New Year.

March - Banlieues Bleues Festival Paris' most important blues festival event in the Seine St Denis suburb.

May - Montmartre Vintage Car Rally.

June - Fête de la Musique - free concert all over Paris on the longest day of the year.

July - Bastille Day Commemorating the uprising that marked the beginning of the French Revolution.

August - Festival Rock en Seine The annual 2-day Festival Rock en Seine.

October - White Night in Paris One night every October many of Paris' libraries, museums and parks stay open all night.

December - New Year's Celebrations with spectacular fireworks.

Where to stay?

Ideally we'd all have a bath tub with a view to Eiffel tower, but in a city of 2.2 million people it's a tough ask. The double-digit arrondissements (districts), with the exception of the 17th and 18th are the more affordable areas. Gare du Nord is a budget travellers area because of its close proximity to Eurostar, but some find it a bit dirty. I have stayed there four times, and never had any problems but if you are looking for a chic area to stay, the double-digit arrondissements are best, you can use the metro to get into the city easily. St Christopher's Inn Canal is the best reviewed hostel in Paris and offers dorms from $20 a night. If you're travelling as a group, hotels are your best bang for your buck. Airbnbs are expensive in Paris.

If you want to experience Parisian nightlife book a hostel along Canal St. Martin. It's the young hipster capital of the city.

Airbnb v Hotels

You can find a lot of cheap eats in Paris. Or do as the Parisians do: buy cheese and baguettes and dine on picnics in the park. You don't really need a kitchen to save money on food in Paris as there's a lot of delicious ready to eat food in the supermarkets. Plus Airbnbs in Paris average out at $157 a night. Hotels are actually cheaper and if a free-breakfast is included, better value.

The cheapest hotel deals are available when you 'blind book'. You don't know the name of the hotel before you book. Use Last Minute Top Secret hotels and you can find a four star hotel from $80 a night in Paris! https://

www.lastminute.com/hotels/france/paris/4-star-top-secret-hotel-in-paris

Hack your Paris Accommodation

Your two biggest expenses when travelling to Paris are accommodation and food. This section is intended to help you cut these costs dramatically before and while you are in Paris.

Hostels are the cheapest accommodation in Paris but there are some creative workarounds to upgrade your stay on the cheap.

Use Time

There are two ways to use time. One is to book in advance. Three months will net you the best deal, especially if your visit coincides with an event. The other is to book on the day of your stay. This is a risky move, but if executed well, you can lay your head in a five-star hotel for a 2-star fee.

Before you travel to Paris, checked for big events using a simple google search 'What's on in Paris', if you find no big events drawing travellers, risk showing up with no accommodation booked (If there are big events on demand exceeds supply and you should avoid using this strategy). Start checking for discount rooms at 11 am using a private browser on booking.com.

Before I go into demand-based pricing, take a moment to think about your risk tolerance. By risk, I am not talking about personal safety. No amount of financial savings is worth risking that. What I am talking about is being inconvenienced. Do you deal well with last-minute changes? Can you roll with the punches or do you freak out if something changes? Everyone is different and knowing yourself is the best way to plan a great trip. If you are someone that likes to have everything pre-planned using demand-based pricing to get cheap accommodation will not work for you. Skip this section and go to blind-booking.

Demand-based pricing

Be they an Airbnb host or hotel manager; no one wants empty rooms. Most will do anything to make some revenue because they still have the same costs to cover whether the room is occupied or not. That's why you will find many hotels drastically slashing room rates for same-day bookings.

How to book five-star hotels for a two-star price

You will not be able to find these discounts when the demand exceeds the supply. So if you're visiting during the peak season, or during an event which has drawn many travellers again don't try this.

On the day of your stay, visit booking.com (which offers better discounts than Kayak and agoda.com). Hotel Tonight individually checks for any last-minute bookings, but they take a big chunk of the action, so the better deals come from booking.com. The best results come from booking between 2 pm and 4 pm when the risk of losing any revenue with no occupancy is most pronounced, so algorithms supporting hotels slash prices. This is when you can find rates that are not within the "lowest publicly visible" rate. To avoid losing customers to other websites, or cheapening the image of their hotel most will only offer the super cheap rates during a two hour window from 2 pm to 4 pm. Two guests will pay 10x difference in price but it's absolutely vital to the hotel that neither knows it.

Takeaway: To get the lowest price book on the day of stay between 2 pm and 4 pm and extend your search radius to include further afield hotels with good transport connections.

How to trick travel Algorithms to get the lowest hotel price

Do not believe anyone who says changing your IP address to get cheaper hotels or flights does NOT work. If you don't believe us, download a Tor Network and search for flights and hotels to one destination using your current IP and then the tor network (a tor browser hits your IP address from algorithms. It is commonly used by hackers). You will receive different prices.

The price you see is a decision made by an algorithm that adjusts prices using data points such as past bookings, remaining capacity, average demand and the probability of selling the room or flight later at a higher price. If booking.com knows you've searched for the area before it will keep the prices high. To circumvent this, you can either use a different IP address from a cafe or airport or data from an international sim. I use a sim from Three, which provides free data in many countries around the world. When you search from a new IP address, most of the time, and particularly near booking you will get a lower price. Sometimes if your sim comes from a 'rich' country, say the UK or USA, you will see higher rates as the algorithm has learnt people from these countries pay more. The solution is to book from a local wifi connection - but a different one from the one you originally searched from.

sHow to get last-minute discounts on owner rented properties

In addition to Airbnb, you can also find owner rented rooms and apartments on www.vrbo.com or HomeAway or a host of others. Nearly all owners renting accommodation will happily give renters a "last-minute" discount to avoid the space sitting empty, not earning a dime.

Go to Airbnb or another platform and put in today's date. Once you've found something you like start the negotiating by asking for a 25% reduction. A sample message to an Airbnb host might read:

Dear HOST NAME,

I love your apartment. It looks perfect for me. Unfortunately, I'm on a very tight budget. I hope you won't be offended, but I wanted to ask if you would be amenable to offering me a 25% discount for tonight, tomorrow and the following day? I see that you aren't booked. I can assure you, I will leave your place exactly the way I found it. I will put bed linen in the washer and ensure everything is clean for the next guest. I would be delighted to bring you a bottle of wine to thank you for any discount that you could offer.

If this sounds okay, please send me a custom offer, and I will book straight away.

YOUR NAME.

In my experience, a polite, genuine message like this, that proposes reciprocity will be successful 80% of the time. Don't ask for more than 25% off, this person still has to pay the bills and will probably say no as your stay will cost them more in bills than they make. Plus starting higher, can offend the owner and do you want to stay somewhere, where you have offended the host?

In Practice

To use either of these methods, you must travel light. Less stuff means greater mobility, everything is faster and you don't have to check-in or store luggage. If you have a lot of luggage, you're going to have fewer of these opportunities to save on accommodation. Plus travelling light benefits the planet - you're buying, consuming, and transporting less stuff.

Blind-booking

If your risk tolerance does not allow for last-minute booking, you can use blind-booking. Many hotels not wanting to cheapen their brand with known low-prices, choose to operate a blind booking policy. This is where you book without knowing the name of the hotel you're going to stay in until you've made the payment. This is also sometimes used as a marketing strategy where the hotel is seeking to recover from past issues. I've stayed in plenty of blind book hotels. As long as you choose 4 or 5 star hotels, you will find them to be clean, comfortable and safe. priceline.com, Hot Rate® Hotels and Top Secret Hotels (operated by lastminute.com) offer the best deals.

Hotels.com Loyalty Program

This is currently the best hotel loyalty program with hotels in Paris. The basic premise is you collect 10 nights and get 1 free. hotels.com price match, so if booking.com has a cheaper price you can get hotel.com, to match. If you intend to travel more than ten nights in a year, its a great choice to get the 11th free.

Don't let time use you.

Rigidity will cost you money. You pay the price you're willing to pay, not the amount it requires a hotel to deliver. Therefore if you're in town for a big event, saving money on accommodation is nearly impossible so in such cases book three months ahead.

The best price performance location in Paris

A room putting Paris's attractions, restaurants, and nightlife within walking distance will save you time on transport. However restaurants and bars do get much cheaper the further you go from famous tourist attractions. You will also get a better idea of the day to day life of a local if you stay in a neighbourhood like the 20th arrondissement. It depends on the Paris you want to experience. For the tourist experience stay in the centre either in a last-minute hotel or Airbnb. For a taste of local life the leafy district of 20th arrondissement is the best you will find. Chopin, Edith Piaf, Proust and Oscar Wilde all lived there at one time. Hôtel Tamaris is a luxurious hotel with rooms from $40 a night in the 20th arrondissement.

INSIDER MONEY SAVING TIP

You can stay for free in a shop frequented by Hemingway and James Joyce. Shakespesre & Co. has hosted over 30,000 "Tumbleweeds" who stay for free in exchange for helping out in the shop and reading and writing. Call or email if you're interested in staying with them for free. Shakespeare & Company and Abbey Bookshop also host free book reading and literary events throughout the year - worth checking out while your in town.

Use our FREE accommodation finder service

Feeling overwhelmed by all the accommodation options? Save yourself stress, hassle and time by using our FREE accommodation finder service.

We pride ourselves on actively helping our readers find the best price-performance accommodation. We normally charge $50 for this service, but for our paid readers it is FREE when you leave an honest review of this book. (Just a few short words like 'Excellent budget tips and insider insights' is all it takes).

So, how do you use the service?

Simply send our Services Manager, Amy Abraham the following information:

1. A screenshot proof of purchase. (Go to your Amazon account, and click orders and make a screenshot of your purchase.)
2. Send a screenshot of your review of the guide on Amazon.
3. And answers to the following questions:

- What's your Budget? (e.g. lowest possible)
- How many are travelling and what are their ages?
- What Approximate location do you desire? (e.g. as close to the centre as possible/ near public transport)
- Do you have a strong dislike of either hostels or Airbnbs?

- If anyone in your group has mobility restrictions/ requires a lift/ no stairs etc?
- Add any details you think are pertinent to your needs.

About Amy and her team

Amy has travelled to over 170 countries personally and has recruited a team of bargain hunters to provide our accommodation finder service.

Send your details via E-mail to Amy Abraham at Amy@supercheapinsiderguides.com

What you'll receive

Amy and her team will work their magic. Within 24 hours you will be sent a list of the top three accommodations for your specific needs prioritised by which one we recommend.

We offer the same service for finding you the cheapest most direct flight. See our cheapest route to Paris for details.

If you would like to follow us on Facebook you can find us here: https://www.facebook.com/SuperCheapInsiderGuides/ . We also accept accommodation search requests via Facebook messenger, just make sure you send the necessary information listed above.

(Please note: If you received this book for free as part of a promotion, we cannot extend this service to you.)

How to be a green tourist in Paris

Paris like other major urban metropolis battles with air pollution; it's important as responsible tourists that we help not hinder Paris. There is a bizarre misconception that you have to spend money to travel in an eco-friendly way. This like, all marketing myths was concocted and hyped by companies seeking to make money off of you. In my experience, anything with eco in front of their names e.g Eco-tours will be triple the cost of the regular tour. Don't get me wrong sometimes its best to take these tours if you're visiting endangered areas, but normally such places have extensive legislation that everyone, including the eco and non-eco tour operators must comply with. The vast majority of ways you can travel eco-friendly are free and even save you money:

- Avoid Bottled Water - get a good water bottle and refill. The water in Paris is safe to drink.
- Thrift shop but check the labels and don't buy polyester clothes - overtime plastic is released into the ocean when we wash polyester.
- Don't put it in a plastic bag, bring a cotton tote with you when you venture out.
- Pack Light - this is one of the best ways to save money. If you find a 5-star hotel for tonight for $10, and you're at an Airbnb or hostel, you can easily pack and upgrade hassle-free. A light pack equals freedom and it means less to wash.
- Travel around Paris on Bikes or e-Scooters or use Public Transportation.
- Car Pool with services like bla bla car or Uber/Lyft share.
- Walk, this is the best way to get to know Paris. You never know what's around the corner.
- Travel Overland - this isn't always viable especially if you only have limited time off work, but where possible avoid flying and if you have to compensate by off-setting or

keeping the rest of your trip carbon-neutral by doing all of the above.

Saving money on Paris Food

Use 'Too Good To Go'

Paris offers plenty of food bargains; if you know where to look. Thankfully the app 'Too Good to Go' is turning visitors into locals by showing them exactly where to find the tastiest deals and simultaneously rescue food that would otherwise be wasted. In Paris you can pick up a $15 buy of baked goods, groceries, breakfast, brunch, lunch or dinner boxes for $2.99. You'll find lots of fish and meat dishes on offer in Paris, which would normally be expensive.

How it works? You pay for a magic bag (essentially a bag of what the restaurant or bakery has leftover) on the app and simply pick it up from the bakery or restaurant during the time they've selected. You can find extremely cheap breakfast, lunch, dinner and even groceries this way. Simply download the app and press 'my current location' to find the deals near you in Paris. https://toogoodtogo.org/en .What's not to love about restaurant quality delicious food thats a quarter of the normal price and helping to drive down food waste?

An oft-quoted parable is 'There is no such thing as cheap food. Either you pay at the cash registry or the doctor's office'. This dismisses the fact that good nutrition is a choice; we all make every-time we eat. Cheap eats are not confined to hotdogs and kebabs. The great thing about using Too Good To Go is you can eat nutritious food cheaply: fruits, vegetables, fish and nut dishes are a fraction of their supermarket cost.

Japan has the longest life expectancy in the world. A national study by the Japanese Ministry of Internal Affairs and Communications revealed that between January and May 2019, a household of two spent on average ¥65,994 a month, that's $10 per person per day on food. You truly don't need to spend a lot to eat nutritious food. That's a marketing gimmick hawkers of overpriced muesli bars want you to believe.

Breakfast

If you stay somewhere with a free breakfast, eat smart. Don't eat sugary cereals or white flour rich pastries if you don't want to be hungry an hour later. Before leaving your hotel or checking out, find some fresh fruit, water, and granola in the fitness centre or coffee in the lobby or business centre. If your hotel doesn't have free breakfast, don't take it. You can always eat cheaper outside. Mich'sandwiches (not a typo, the name of the cafe) has the best cheap breakfast we found. Here you can pick up crepes for less than $2.

Visit supermarkets at discount times.

You can get a 50 per cent discount around 5 pm at the Carrefour supermarkets on fresh produce. The cheaper the supermarket, the less discounts you will find, so check Carrefour's at 5 pm instead of discount supermarkets. Some items are also marked down due to sell-by date after the lunchtime rush so its also worth to check in around 3 pm.

Use delivery services on the cheap.

Take advantage of local offers on food delivery services. Most platforms including Uber Eats and Foodora offer $10 off the first order in Paris.

SNAPSHOT: How to enjoy a $1,000 trip to Paris for $200

(full breakdown at the end of the guide)

Stay	https://www.airbnb.com/rooms/5621063?s=51 Private room on airbnb - https://www.airbnb.com/rooms/13873474?s=51 $19 in the city https://www.airbnb.com/rooms/5621063?s=51 or use our accommodation finder service.
Eat	Croissants, pastries, all-you-can-eats, supermarket bread, cheese and wine
Move	Metro, bike, walk $8
See	Free museums, Louvre, churches, Eiffel Tower, monuments
Total	US$200

Unique bargains I love in Paris

Paris has the reputation of being among the most luxurious and expensive cities in the world. Fortunately, some of the best things in life are free (or almost free). Eat street food like crepes and from bakeries or supermarkets. Buy an eclair from La Galette des Moulins in Montmartre (cheaper and better eclairs than the fancy well known ones) and after eating the eclair, the first thing you should do when you arrive is check http://www.freeinparis.com/free-paris/ to see what free events are on.

Avoid staying close to the city centre/ Eiffel Tower. Everything (like accommodation and dining) is more expensive the closer you get. n.

Paris has some of the best flea markets; there are bargains to be found if you don't mind sifting through endless clothing rails. The

St-Ouen Flea Market (Porte de Clignacourt, 18th Arr.) is the largest of its kind in the world and while it markets itself as an antique market, you will find many amazing second hand designer pieces. Porte de Vanves Flea Market (Blvd. Lefebvre, 14th Arr.) is also great for clothes. Visit rue Cler - a cool little market street with an amazing and cheap cheese shop: La Fromagerie. Even the most reluctant bargain hunter can be successful in Paris. There's so much to see and do cheaply that you will be planning your second visit.

How to use this book

Google and Tripadvisor are your on-the-go guides while travelling, a travel guide adds the most value during the planning phase, and if you're without wifi. Always download the google map for your destination - having an offline map will make using this guide much more comfortable. For ease of use, we've set the book out the way you travel starting with arriving, how to get around, then on to the money-saving tips. The tips we ordered according to when you need to know the tip to save money, so free tours and combination tickets feature first. We prioritised the rest of the tips by how much money you can save and then by how likely it was that you would be able to find the tip with a google search. Meaning those we think you could find alone are nearer the bottom. I hope you find this layout useful. If you have any ideas about making super cheap guides easy to use, please email me philgattang@gmail.com . Now let's get started with juicing the most pleasure from your trip to Paris with the least possible money.

OUR SUPER CHEAP TIPS
Arriving

From the airport
The cheapest way from the Charles De Gaulle airport is with the ARATP bus 350 (€6; 70 minutes; every 30 minutes, 5.30am to 11pm). The bus Links the airport with Gare de l'Est in northern Paris.

If you fly into **Orly airport**, the bus costs €12 to the centre of Paris. It takes about 35 minutes. The only other option is Uber which costs 30 euros.

INSIDER MONEY SAVING TIP

Cheap Eurostar
Booking six months in advance on eurostar.com can net you tickets for $35 from London to Paris.

Getting around

Bike
Paris is a lovely city to cycle. Like a growing number of cities around the world, Paris has an established bike-sharing program: velib. You pay a fee of 1,70 EUR for a day-ticket or 8 Euro for a week ticket. You can use any bicycle from the velib network.

E-scooters:
Paris has e-scooters (Lime, Bird and Dott are the main providers) but you can only ride them on roads and bike lanes, if you're caught on the footpath it's a fine of €130.

The metro
Paris is one of the most well-connected cities in the world. It costs 1.90€ for a single ticket to ride the metro but its cheaper to buy 10 tickets, a carnet ["car-nay"] for 14.90€. Avoid rush hour (4pm - 6pm). Keep your ticket at all times, random inspections

are common and you will be fined if you can't show a valid ticket. If you're travelling alone, avoid these stations at night: Châtelet–Les Halles and its corridors; Château Rouge in Montmartre; Gare du Nord; Strasbourg St-Denis; Réaumur Sébastopol; and Montparnasse Bienvenüe. Beware of your surrounding and keep an eye on your belongings.

Paris is a city that rewards those who explore it by foot. Pack good walking shoes and walk.

The Paris Métro

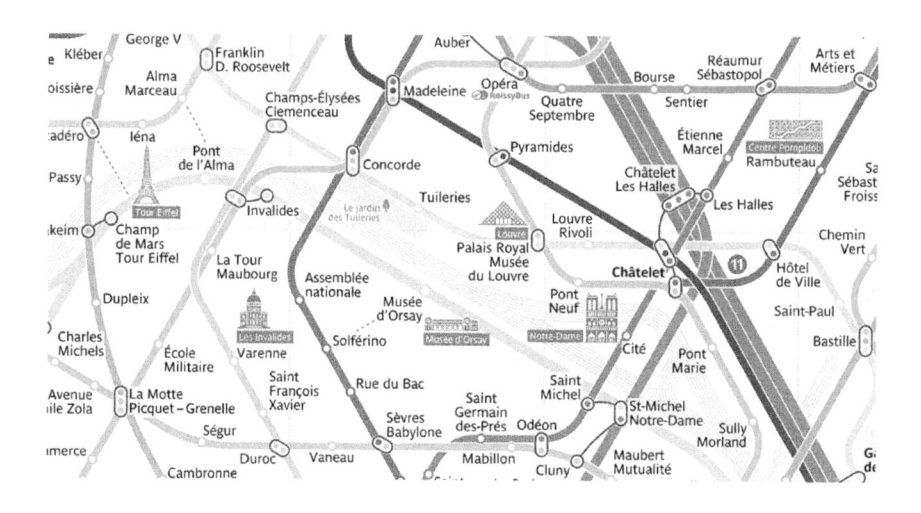

Start with this free tour

Forget exploring Paris by wandering around aimlessly. Always start with a free organised tour. Nothing compares to local advice, especially when travelling on a budget. I gleamed many of our super cheap tips from local guides and locals in general, so start with a organised tour to get your bearings and ask for their recommendations for the best cheap eats, the best bargains, the best markets, the best place for a particular street eat. Perhaps some of it will be repeated from this guide, but it can't hurt to ask, especially if you have specific needs or questions. At the end you should leave an appropriate tip (usually around $5), but nobody bats an eye lid if you are unable or unwilling to do so, tell them you will leave a good review and always give them a little gift from home - I always carry small Vienna fridge magnets and I always tip the $5, but it is totally up to you.

I pre-booked the Paris Greeters tour (www.greeters.Paris) where you get to see Paris through local eyes for these two- to three-hours. https://greeters.paris/en/meet-a-greeter/ (you must book at least four weeks in advance)

You can also do over 12 different free walking tours depending on what you're interested in: https://freetoursbyfoot.com/paris-tours/

A note on paying for tours

The only time paying for a tour is worth it, is when you couldn't reach the place without the tour (e.g you need a boat), or when the tour is about the same price as the attraction entry. Otherwise you can do a range of self-guided tours using gpsmycity.com for FREE.

INSIDER MONEY SAVING TIP

Try Geocaching

This is where you hunt for hide-and-seek containers. You need a mobile device to follow the GPS clues in Paris. A typical cache is a small, waterproof container with a logbook where you can leave a message or see various trinkets left by other cache hunters. Build your own treasure hunt by discovering geocaches in Paris. www.geocaching.com

COMBO PASSES

Attraction aficionados can save money with combo passes in Paris. There are a couple of different options:

1. the Paris Pass
2. Paris Passlib'
3. the Paris Museum pass

Paris Pass
It worked out cheaper to just pay for the attractions al a carte, buy groupons, buy discounted tickets etc than to buy the Paris Pass. In my opinion it is just a collection of existing passes and tickets put into an envelope, and sold for far more than the cost of the individual components.

Paris Passlib'
€109 for two days of unlimited public transport in zones 1 to 3, a Paris Museum Pass, a one-hour boat cruise, and a one-day bus tour with L'Open Tour.

ARC DE TRIOMPHE : 12€
+ CENTRE POMPIDOU : 14€
+ MUSÉE DU QUAI BRANLY : 9€
+ MUSÉE DU LOUVRE : 15€
+ TOURS DE NOTRE-DAME : 10€
+ MUSÉE D'ORSAY : 12€
+ PANTHÉON : 8,50€
+ MUSÉE RODIN : 10€
+ SAINTE-CHAPELLE : 10€
+ CHÂTEAU DE VERSAILLES : 18€

= 118,50 €

The Paris Museum Pass
Offers the best bang for your buck. Costing €48 for two days with potential savings of €70 if you visit all the included attractions - see below parismuesumpass.com plus you can bypass long ticket queues.

Note: There are long lines for most attractions even with the Passes. And at several attractions it was faster in the prepaid or paid lines. Go early to avoid queuing.

Can you already get in for free? For students and seniors with valid ID; children and students who are EU citizens under 26 admission to most museums is free.

INSIDER HISTORICAL INSIGHT

Celtic people first settled Paris giving it the name Parisii. The name Parisii was later shortened in 508 A.D. to Paris.

Visit these amazing free Museums

Musée d'Orsay

To make sure everybody has access to culture many of Paris' top museums can be accessed for free and ALL are worth a visit. Here are the best of the crop:

Always free
- Visit the permanent collections of Paris' *musées municipaux* (www.Paris.fr/musees) for free
- Pavillon de l'Arsenal
- Musée du Parfum - perfume museums with free guided tours.

Free first Sunday of the month (during specific months)
- Arc de Triomphe November to March
- Basilique de St-Denis November to March
- Château de Versailles November to March

- Cité de l'Architecture et du Patrimoine
- Conciergerie November to March
- Musée des Arts et Métiers Also free every Thursday from 6pm
- Musée des Impressionnismes Giverny
- Musée d'Orsay
- Musée du Louvre October to March
- Musée du Quai Branly
- Musée Guimet des Arts Asiatiques
- Musée National d'Art Moderne Within the Centre Pompidou
- Musée National du Moyen Âge Aka Musée de Cluny
- Musée National Eugène Delacroix
- Musée National Gustave Moreau
- Musée National Picasso
- Musée Rodin October to March
- Panthéon November to March
- Musée de la Chasse et de la Nature
- Musée de l'Histoire de l'Immigration
- Musée de l'Orangerie
- Crypte Arhcéologique de Notre Dame is free every Sunday morning between 10am-1pm (but due to the recent fire is closed until 2022)
- Cognacq-jay musée: A small museum dedicated to the art and design of the old regime, and particularly the 18th century, housed in an old apartment,

BEWARE: Do be careful in the Queues. They are snakingly long and this present a great opportunity for pickpockets.

💡 INSIDER INSIGHT

You'd be in the Louvre 35 days straight to spend 30 seconds at each artwork!

Cheap entry

Queue Free Louvre

Home to Leonardo da Vinci 1503 painted 'Mona Lisa'. The Louvre is divided into three wings over four floors. The main entrance and ticket windows are covered by the glass pyramid designed IM Pei. Enter the Louvre complex via the underground shopping centre Carrousel du Louvre - 99 rue de Rivoli to avoid the queues and pickpockets who lurk around them.

Climb the Eiffel Tower

This was the world's tallest building when it was built in 1889 for the World Fair. It was supposed to be a temporary structure, but is still here 130 years later. The views from the different observation decks are breathtaking. It is open daily from 9.30am-11.45pm admission €4.50 (1st floor), €7.80 (2nd floor), €11.50 (top).

Visit Versailles on the cheap

Versailles is Louis XIV's gilded palace. It's prolific game attracted France's Kings and eventually lead to its construction. It is an immense, 18th-century palace with gilded apartments, chandeliered Hall of Mirrors & fountain show. The cheapest and easiest way to get to Versailles is by Paris RER train costing 3.65€.

Over five million people visit Versailles annually. Follow these three tips for the most enjoyable experience:

1. Arrive early morning and avoid Tuesday, Saturday and Sundays - the busiest days.
2. Pre-purchase tickets on the château's website www.chateau-versailles.fr to avoid LONG queues

3. Download the free app from the website to give you a free audio guide of Versailles

Disneyland Paris on the cheap

The cheapest way to visit Disneyland Paris is to stay in one of the partner hotels: Explorers, Magic Circus, Dream Castle or the Kyrad they are all next to each other, there is a free shuttle that collects and drops off every 10-15min from morning until the parks close. Kyriad is usually the cheapest but doesn't have a pool. Entry to the Disney Village is free. If you want to enter the Park, buy your ticket for the park on the website to save 20 euros.

Do a river cruise on the cheap

Vedettes du Pont Neuf is impossible to beat on price. The ticket costs 12 euros, you get a 2 euro discount available on their site anytime making it 10 euros.

Climb to Sacré-Cœur

This Landmark hilltop white basilica was completed in 1914. Its free to go inside to marvel at the interior mosaics and stained-glass windows. Afterwards walk around pretty Montmartre with its many tourist souvenir shops and cafes.

Visit Galeries Lafayette

We are not going to suggest you spend all your money at this high-end department store but we do suggest you go there to marvel at the Art Nouveau stained-glass dome. After go to the 7th floor to watch a French haute-couture 30-minutes fashion show (advance booking only **via email only** - haussmann.galerieslafayette.com). Finish off by going to the top floor to enjoy gorgeous views of Paris from the terrace (open in summer only).

Church Hop

Not only exceptional architecturally and historically, Paris's churches contain exquisite art, artefacts and other priceless treasures. Best of all, entry to general areas within them is, in most cases, free. You must visit 13th century Sainte-Chapelle to see its mind-blowing stained glass windows.

You can still visit Cathédrale Notre-Dame de Paris from outside even after the fire. They began building Notre-Dame in 1163 and completed 170 years later, it's a prime example of gothic style, with its rose windows and massive flying buttresses.

Eglise St-Séverin is one of Paris's most beautiful small churches, a late gothic gem from the days when medieval power and learning were concentrated in the Latin Quarter. Frills of carved gargoyles adorn the outside.

Visit Icons

Père Lachaise Cemetery

Père Lachaise Cemetery is a vast tree-lined burial site with many famous people buried here including Oscar Wilde, Jim Morrison & Maria Callas, Edith Piaf and Sandra Bernhardt. Open daily from 8am-7pm.

Go Thrift shopping

Thrift stores also known as charity shops or second hand shops are full of chic bargains in Paris if you know where to look. Marais is nice for vintage and thrift shopping. Also Boulevard Saint-Michel has awesome places. If you like flea markets, Marché aux Puces is a MUST!

Google for the most expensive area in Paris, they are a little outside the city. Then put the American term Thrift store into Google Maps. Start with the most expensive areas and work your way through until the middle-tier ones. You will be surprised what you find in Paris with a bit of patience!

Pack a picnic

The cost of eating out can quickly add up. For a meal that doesn't break the bank, prepare your own picnic to enjoy in a park with a blanket and a bottle of fizz. Picnics are a favourite pastime of Parisians, so grab some wine cheese and bread and head to the bank of the seine, canal saint martin, or almost any parc and just enjoy the the scenery.

The French capital has some of the best-kept parks in the world, and it doesn't cost a thing to pull up one of the free chairs and relax for a while. Jardin du Carrousel before Le Louvre is adorned with endless statues, Jardin du Luxembourg lies in front of a palace of the same name, while the view of the Eiffel Tower from Parc du Champ de Mars is unforgettable. It is my absolute favourite garden in Paris. Created by regent Queen Marie de Médici in 1612 to complement her new residence Palais du Luxembourg. It has been the seat of the French Senate since 1958.

Buttes Chaumont Parc is one of the most beautiful parks in Paris. Grab a bottle of wine (and an opener) then head to the park and lay on a blanket, there's really no better way to waste a few hours.

Parc floral de Paris is a gorgeous park filled with flowers. It's 2€ entry, but worth it.

Explore Street art

Colorful murals and graffiti art are displayed throughout the city. Murals sometimes cover up entire buildings and symbolize recent and historical events and topics. Here are the best places to spot them:

- Oberkampf. This colourful neighbourhood is renowned for its vibrant walls and range of high profile street artists.
- Belleville.
- Rue Germaine Taillefaire.
- 13th Arrondissement.
- L'Aerosol.

Explore the markets

Marché Bastille

Markets are a fun and eye-opening plunge into local culture and, unless you succumb to the persistent vendors, it will cost you nothing. You must visit the oldest food market in Paris: Marché des Enfants Rouges. Then go to the lively one: Marché d'Aligre. The best food market is: Marché Bastille. The most traditional one: Marché Mouffetard. Visit the Modern: Les Halles, Paris's central fresh food market. It was demolished in 1971 and replaced into a modern shopping mall built largely underground and directly connected to the metro.

The most famous flea market in Paris is at Porte de Clignancourt, officially called Les Puces de Saint-Ouen, but locals call it Les Puces (The Fleas). It covers seven hectares and is the largest antique market in the world.

Hunt for rare first editions

San-Francisco Book Co is an English book store in Paris. If you take the time to search, you're certain to find some gems.
Address: 17 Rue Monsieur le Prince

Moulin Rouge

Moulin Rouge is a vastly overpriced tourist trap. Tickets start at $120 and there's no work around. Instead you could go to watch Free Comedy at Laughing Matters at La Java
Address: 105 rue du Faubourg du Temple, Paris 10th.

If you are yearning to see a cabernet show in Paris, go around the corner to La Nouvelle Eve. It's a smaller venue so it feels like you're more involved. Seats cost €59 which includs half a bottle of champagne

Do Free yoga

Working out in Paris can expensive cost 15€-25€ per session, which can quickly add up. You can find free yoga at - http://www.freeinParis.com/affordable-yoga-Paris/

People watch outside a café

The French are a passionate race and watching them go about their daily lives is one of the best things you can do in Paris. Get yourself comfy outside one of the city's omnipresent cafés, sit back and watch the world go by.

Free entertainment

In the summer you can watch a free film under the stars in Parc de la Villlette (www.lavillette.com).

If you like Jazz, visit Cave du 38 Riv'Jazz in Le Marais they have free admission on Mondays, Thursdays and Fridays.

Escape the crowds

If you are easily overwhelmed by crowds visit the obvious attractions as early as possible, peak people flow is 11 am to 5 pm so get up early to enjoy the attractions serenely. Luckily Paris also has many hidden gems that aren't commercialised or too crowded most of the time. Here are the best:

1. Rue Cremieux is a small pedestrian street that's lined with houses painted in bright colours. Visit at noon when the sun lights up the brightly colored houses.
2. The Parc des Buttes-Chaumont was created out of an abandoned quarry. It opened in 1867 and is a great place to relax away from the crowds.
3. The terrace at Printemps Department store offers amazing panoramic views of Paris. Take the elevator to Cafe Déli-Cieux.
4. The often overlooked Rue Mouffetard is one of the best market streets in the whole of Paris and relatively quiet before 10am.
5. Monet's Garden in Giverny
6. The castles in the Loire Valley
7. You can do a day trip by train to Brussels (1.5 hours each way) or Luxembourg (2.5 hours each way).
8. La Promenade Plantée is an old subway station/stop turned into a beautiful 4Km walking park that takes you through several neighbourhoods and is amazing.
9. Parc sceaux: another gorgeous park with a gorgeous chateau. The best cherry blossoms in Paris area.

Food and drink tips

Appreciate the local flavours without paying gourmet restaurant prices.
Go to supermarkets and bakeries! Buy meat, cheese & bread in supermarkets. Everything will be delicious. Avoid the touristy looking bakeries and try to wander down a sidestreet and find a smaller one catering to locals.

Lunch menu's
Lots of restaurants also have lunch menus on weekdays so you can get a 2 course meal for 10-15€pp.

Download the app Dojo
It tells you price range and distance for Paris restaurants.

Middle Ages pâtisserie
Le Moulin de la Vierge on rue Saint Dominique is a pâtisserie shop that's been open since the Middle Ages.

Best bang for your buck all-you-can-eat's

Paris offers an array of bargain all you can eat restaurants with lunches for $15. These are the best three:

1. Buffet Sentier - the all you can eat sushi lunch includes desserts which is a real plus

2. Dim Sum House Restaurant. They offer an all-you-can-eat menu in which you can find all of the

3. Restaurant Hao Hao Sushi. Very good all-you-can-eat Japanese restaurant. Service is fast and everything is delicious.

All you can eat buffets are a great way to stock on on nutritious food while travelling. Dishes like fish are normally expensive, but here you can chow down on your omega 3's for much less. I know friends who take Tupperware with them to take some snacks away, personally I don't as its not ethical and karma is real. Don't drink much water or eat bread and you'll get more than your money's worth.

Eat at the cafe under napoleons tomb
For just for 11€ per person you can eat under napoleons tomb. The cafe is only open from 11-2, it's run by nuns and all the money goes to help the needy. To enter, if you're standing in front of the building it's around the left side, pass the flower vendor.

Nightlife

Prime Parisian streets for partying are:

- Rue Princesse, 6e Student and sports bars.
- Rue Vieille du Temple, 4e Marais cocktail of gay bars and chic cafes.
- Rue Oberkampf, 11e Edgy urban hang-outs.
- Rue de Lappe, 11e Boisterous Bastille bars and clubs.
- Rue de la Butte aux Cailles, 13e Village atmosphere and fun local haunts.

Here are the cheapest places to drink:

Marlusse et lapin
14 Rue Germain Pilon
Hidden secret of Montmartre. Good selection of Belgian beers for €5 each.

Pop In · Bar
105 Rue Amelot
One of the friendliest places in Paris, home of the Parisian indie crowd. Cheap drinks and free gigs every night & open mic sessions on Sundays.

Zero Zero
89 Rue Amelot
happy hour drinks from 4 euros. Very small space for dancing.

Le Viaduc:
Located right by Gare de Lyon, they have almost everything on happy hour is 3€ and HH is every day 17h- 0200. There isn't another bar in Paris as cheap as this.

If you are looking for a wild night out, check out Rue de lappe and Rue de Mouffetard. Rue de lappe is located in Bastille and it's jammed packed with bars that's stay open all night, the party really never stops. Rue de Mouffetard is in the Latin Quarter it's slightly less wild, but its still a great time if you're trying to get your party on.

Drink prices can be crazily expensive in Paris. Pre-drink by enjoying a bottle of wine somewhere green with friends before bar hopping to cut costs.

Not super cheap but loved

Atelier des lumieres

One of the most moving art experiences you can have have ever had. The work of Klimt comes alive and unfolded with drama and emotion. It costs 14.50 to enter.

Don't leave Paris without seeing (at least from outside)

Eiffel Tower
Gustave Eiffel's iconic, wrought-iron 1889 tower, with steps and elevators to observation decks.

Louvre Museum
Former historic palace housing huge art collection, from Roman sculptures to da Vinci's Mona Lisa.

Notre-Dame de Paris
Towering, 13th-century cathedral with flying buttresses & gargoyles, setting for Hugo's novel. You can sign a book of hope for its refurbishment.

Arc de Triomphe
Iconic triumphal arch built to commemorate Napoleon's victories, with an observation deck.

Champs-Élysées
Famed route of landmarks such as the Louvre, Tuileries & Arc de Triomphe plus shops & restaurants.

Palace of Versailles
Immense, 18th-century palace with gilded apartments, chandeliered Hall of Mirrors & fountain show.

Sacré-Cœur
Iconic, domed white church, completed in 1914, with interior mosaics, stained-glass windows & crypt.

Place de la Concorde

Major public square, scene of executions, decorated with fountains, statues & an Egyptian obelisk.

Musée d'Orsay
Major 19th- & 20th-century European art collections housed in a monumental, former railway station.

Les Invalides
Series of army museums including a church & the tombs of many famed officers, including Napoleon.

Champ de Mars
Landscaped park with paths & trees, bird life, extensive lawns & a children's play area.

Saint-Germain-des-Prés
Saint-Germain-des-Prés is one of the four administrative quarters of the 6th arrondissement.

Rmn-Grand Palais
Art nouveau hall with domed glass roof, built in 1900, hosting exhibitions and cultural events.

Tour Montparnasse
Modern 210m tower with panoramic views from roof terrace and 56th-floor observation deck.

Place de la Bastille
The July Column rises above this iconic square's bars & cafes, former site of the Bastille prison.

Conciergerie
Gothic, riverside fortress & French Revolution prison, housing Marie Antoinette's former cell.

Palais Garnier
Italian-style opera house with ceiling painted by Chagall & library museum in 19th-century building.

Place des Vosges

Oldest planned square in Paris, lined with trees and red brick houses, built by Henri IV in 1612.

Musée de l'Orangerie
Museum with 20th-century European art collection, showcasing 8 of Monet's water lilies murals.

Canal Saint-Martin
The Canal Saint-Martin is a 4.6 km long canal in Paris, connecting the Canal de l'Ourcq to the river Seine.

Bastille
The Bastille was a fortress in Paris, known formally as the Bastille Saint-Antoine.

Pont Neuf
Arched stone bridge, opened in 1607, with 2 spans & a bronze, equine statue of King Henri IV.

Rue de Rivoli
Rue de Rivoli is one of the most famous commercial streets whose shops include the most fashionable names in the world.

Jardin des plantes
Vast park with plant species grown in botanical & alpine gardens & restored 19th-century hothouses.

Musée Rodin
18th-century mansion & sculpture garden displaying Rodin's influential works, such as The Thinker.

Musée Picasso
17th-century building holding 5,000 artworks by Pablo Picasso, his own art collection & archive.Pont des Arts

Scenic bridge crossing the Seine
Picturesque bridge over the Seine connecting the Louvre & the Institut de France.

Palais-Royal

Palace & gardens with 17th-century arcades of shops & Daniel Buren's striped columns in courtyard.

Parc de la Villette
Wide lawns with sculptures and fountains in urban park with a museum, a cinema and a music complex.

Enjoy your first Day for under $20

Sculpture on the Arc de Triomphe

Start early, at the Eiffel Tower, Paris' most recognisable landmark. After your selfies, stroll up the banks of the River Seine to Place de la Concorde. Enjoy views of the Champs Elysées and LArc de Triomphe. Relax with some shop brought cheese and wine in Jardin du Carrousel, then visit one of the world's most famous museums, Museé du Louvre (free if you're under 26 and from the EU) After the Louvre walk down Rue de Rivoli. Turn onto Rue St. Martin and search for bargains in thrift stores. Just across the Seine on Ile de la Cité is where the Notre Dame Cathedral stands proud and this is a must-see even though it is being reconstructed after the fire. Walk back up to Place de la Concorde and stroll down the Champs Elyseés. Fill your belly at Breizh Café a delicious cheap creperie. At 10pm the Eiffel tower sparkles for 10 minutes and every hour after until 1am - don't miss it!

Websites to save you Money

1. **TalkTalkbnb.com** - Here you stay for free when you teach the host your native language
2. Rome2Rio.com - the go to site for good travel prices on train, bus, planes etc. Especially good for paths less travelled.
3. GoEuro.com - the best travel site in Europe.
4. couchsurfing.com - stay for free with a local - always check reviews.
5. trustedhousesitter.com - always check reviews
6. booking.com - now sends you vouchers for discounts in the city when you book through them
7. blablacar.com - travel in car with locals already going to your destination
8. airbnb.com for both accommodation and experiences.
9. hostelbookers.com - book hostels
10. https://www.discoverwalks.com/tour/city/Paris-walking-tours/ - free walking tour
11. http://en.Parismuseumpass.com/ - entry to musuems totalling $150 for $50
12. https://www.ratp.fr/en/titres-et-tarifs/airport-tickets - bus to the airport $10
13. https://www.thefork.com/best-promotions+Paris - restaurant deals
14. https://www.gpsmycity.com/gps-tour-guides/Paris-488.html - self guided tours in Paris
15. https://www.yelp.com/search?cflt=thrift_stores&find_loc=Paris - 10 best thrift stores.
16. www.bonjourparis.com - a weekly whats on.
17. www.hipparis.com - daily listings of gallery openings

Need to Know

Currency: Euro

Language: French

Money: Widely available ATMs.

Visas: http://www.doyouneedvisa.com/

Time: GMT + 1

When to Go

High Season: July and August.

Shoulder: May, April, June

Low Season: September to May.

Important Numbers

113 Ambulance

112 Police

Watch to understand the History

Paris's history is fascinating. There are tons of documentaries. This is great https://www.youtube.com/watch?v=-64kHmCJGMA

Cheapest route to Paris from America

The cheapest way to Paris is from NYC - booking one-way tickets reduces the cost. Level is the cheapest operator for $113. I specialise in finding cheap flights, so if you need help finding a cheap flight simply review this book and send me an email. philgtang@gmail.com (Please send me a screenshot of your review - with your flight hacking request). I aim to reply to you within 12 hours. If it's an urgent request mark the email URGENT in the subject line and I will endeavour to reply ASAP.

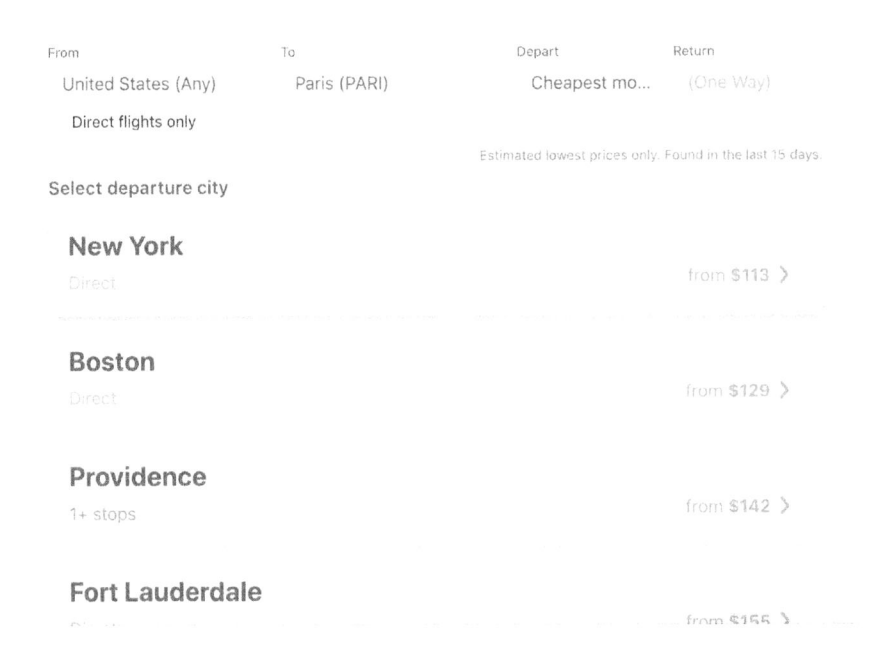

From	To	Depart	Return
United States (Any)	Paris (PARI)	Cheapest mo...	(One Way)

Direct flights only

Estimated lowest prices only. Found in the last 15 days.

Select departure city

New York
Direct — from $113 ›

Boston
Direct — from $129 ›

Providence
1+ stops — from $142 ›

Fort Lauderdale
— from $155 ›

Mains under 5 euros

Fill your stomach without emptying your wallet by trying these local restaurants with mains under $8.

(Download the offline map on google maps, (instructions 1. go to app 2. select offline apps in the left sidebar 3. go to the area you want to download 4. click download). Then simply type the restaurant names in to navigate, star them so you can see where the cheap eats are when you're out and about to avoid wasting your money at hyped tourist joints)

Breizh Café
Cheap delicious Crêperie

Bistro Victoiries
Late-night French food on the cheap.

Krishna Bhavan Restaurant
Vegetarian cheap Indian.

A La Biche Au Bois
Cheaper than most Parisian bistros and the food is better.

Chez Gladines
Great food and huge portions! (beware, you REALLY have to be hungry to finish most of the dishes!)

Higuma
Food was good and cheap, friendly enough people

Chez Shen
local Chinese place, better than affordable and the moment.

Happy Nouilles

Delicious, inexpensive, and fairly quick.

Urfa Durum
Fantastic, authentic, cheap Kurdish sandwich. I recommend the lamb.

Pizza Populare = 5€ pizzas

Le Comptoir de l'Arc next to the Arc de Triomphe for good lunch/dinner for around €12 (v. authentic experience, only open on weekdays).

Cartouche Café
A small french bistro near bercy village. Chalkboard menu that changes daily, incredibly delicious in EVERY sense of the word. (if you go get the chocolate kitsu for dessert you will not regret squeezing it in).

Happy nouille
A Chinese soup noodle place, tiny yet efficient. They hand pull noodles for every bowl so you're getting fresh noodles everytime.

Avoid these tourist traps or scams

Scams and trickery are the scourge of a traveler's budget and unfortunately scams abound in Paris, and particularly near the attractions. Beware of extremely helpful strangers, distraction thefts are very common. If you are at all in doubt of someone's intention say 'No French, No English' and walk on. People can't con you if they can't speak to you.

'Found' Gold ring
A gypsy will offer you a found ring. Avoid this is a long-con.

Museum pickpockets
See the Mona Lisa without getting pickpocketed. Organised gangs operate around museum queues. Don't keep stuff in your back pockets and keep your bag where you can see it. Goes for using the metro too.

The string / bracelet scam
People will try to put a bracelet on you. If you let them weave it on your arm, they will tie it on so tight you won't be able to easily pull it off, and then then will demand money.

Basic Phrases

Merci, which means thank you will be appreciated by servers.

English – detected	French
Hello	Bonjour
How much?	Combien?
Yes	Oui
No	Non
Discount?	Remise?
Can you do cheaper?	Pouvez-vous faire moins cher?
Where is the bus?	Où est le bus?
Thank you	Je vous remercie
Goodbye	Au revoir

Getting Out

Bus

Flixbus
Booking ahead can save you up to 98% of the cost of the ticket. You can do to a favourite of destinations in France and further afield for as little as $3.

Car share

BlaBlaCar is also used here - you can share a car to Brussels for $5 - blablacar.com

Plane

At the time of Transavia are offering the cheapest flights

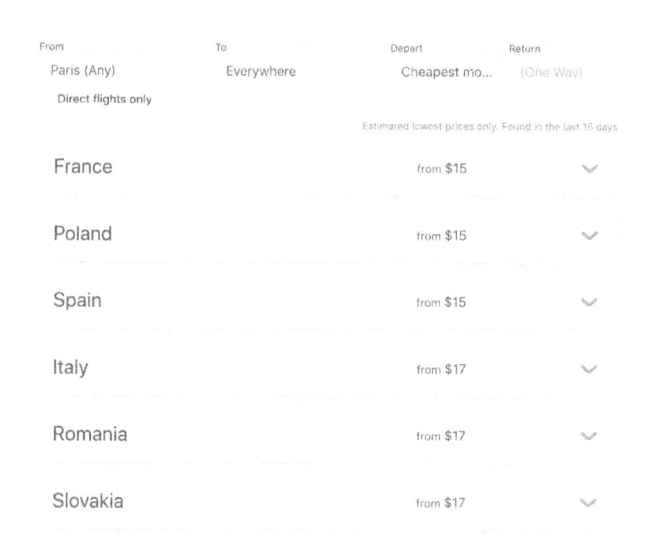

From	To	Depart	Return
Paris (Any)	Everywhere	Cheapest mo...	(One Way)
Direct flights only			

Estimated lowest prices only. Found in the last 15 days.

France	from $15	⌄
Poland	from $15	⌄
Spain	from $15	⌄
Italy	from $17	⌄
Romania	from $17	⌄
Slovakia	from $17	⌄

onwards. Take advantage of discounts and specials. Sign up for e-newsletters from local carriers including Transavia to learn about special fares. Be careful with cheap airlines, most will allow hand-luggage only, and some charge for anything that is not a backpack. Check their websites before booking if you need to take luggage.

RECAP: How to have a $1,000 trip to Paris on a $200 budget

Blind book Five star hotels
The cheapest hotel deals are available when you 'blind book'. You don't know the name of the hotel before you book. Use Last Minute Top Secret hotels and you can find a four star hotel from $80 a night in Paris! https://www.lastminute.com/hotels/france/paris/4-star-top-secret-hotel-in-paris

Pick-up Cheap food
Install the 'Too Good To Go' app to get amazing food super cheap. Potential saving $150.

Restaurant deals / supermarket food
Nearly every restaurant in Paris offers a midday menu for lunch at around 12.90€ If you're on a budget, but like eating out, consider doing your dining in the daytime. Potential saving $100.

Go to museums/ attractions on their free days
Get cultured for free, or for cheap, by knowing the gallery and museum discount days. The average traveller spends $180 on museums in Paris but there's no need to spend a dime if you time your trip to visit on the free days. Potential saving $180.

Drink outdoors with friends
Paris is super green and the best way to experience the city is to buy a couple of beers from a supermarket and en-

joy them somewhere green, or near the river. outdoor public spaces for a few drinks with friends. A beer costs around $8 in a bar. Potential savings on drinks $100 - hey you're on vacation!

Book Ahead
Book six weeks ahead for the lowest prices on outward buses and flights. Potential savings: $100

Personal Cost Breakdown

	How	Cost normally	Cost when following suggested tip
How I got from the airport to the city	Bus - ARATP bus 350	$40 Taxi	$6
Where I stayed	Hostel - St Christopher's Inn Canal	Hotels are upwards of $150 a night.	$60 for three nights with free breakfast.
Tastiest street foods I ate and cost	Crepes, pastries, cheese, wine, baguettes, all-you-can eat sushi	You can experience gourmet Paris without the price tag just shop for cheese, wine and bread at the supermarkets.	$8 average per meal
How I got around	Bike	There are tons of cycle lanes making cycling easy, cheap and maximising sightseeing opportunities.	$8 for the week
What I saw and paid	Free museums, churches, monuments, thrift shops, Atelier des lumieres	If you time your visit right you can save $200 on museums in Paris. If not make sure you enjoy lots of free tours!	$14.50 on the Atelier des lumieres
My onward flight	Eurostar to London	Book in advance for cheap tickets	$25
My Total costs	US$200		US$200

The secret to saving HUGE amounts of money when travelling to Paris is...

Your mindset. Money is an emotional topic, if you associate words like cheapskate, Miser (and its £9.50 to go into Charles Dickens London house, oh the Irony) with being thrifty when travelling you are likely to say 'F-it' and spend your money needlessly because you associate pain with saving money. You pay now for an immediate reward. Our brains are prehistoric; they focus on surviving day to day. Travel companies and hotels know this and put trillions into making you believe you will be happier when you spend on their products or services. Our poor brains are up against outdated programming and an onslaught of advertisements bombarding us with the message: spending money on travel equals PLEASURE. To correct this carefully lodged propaganda in your frontal cortex you need to imagine your future self.

Saving money does not make you a cheapskate. It makes you smart. How do people get rich? They invest their money. They don't go out and earn it; they let their money earn more money. So every time you want to spend money, imagine this: while you travel your money is working for you, not you for money. While you sleep the money you've invested is going up and up. That's a pleasure a pricey entrance fee can't give you. Thinking about putting your money to work for you tricks your brain into believing you are not withholding pleasure from yourself, you are saving your money to invest so you can go to even more amazing places. You are thus turning thrifty travel into a pleasure fueled sport.

When you've got money invested - If you want to splash your cash on a first-class airplane seat - you can. I can't tell you how to invest your money, only that you should. Saving $20 on taxi's doesn't seem like much but over time you could be saving upwards of $15,000 a year, which is a deposit for a house which you can rent on Airbnb to finance more travel. Your brain making money looks like your brain on cocaine, so tell yourself saving money is making money.

Scientists have proved that imagining your future self is the easiest way to associate pleasure with saving money. You can download FaceApp — which will give you a picture of what you will look like older and greyer, or you can take a deep breath just before spending money and ask yourself if you will regret the purchase later.

The easiest ways to waste money travelling are:

Getting a taxi. The solution to this is to always download the google map before you go. Many taxi drivers will drive you around for 15 minutes when the place you were trying to get to is a 5-minute walk… remember while not getting an overpriced taxi to tell yourself, 'I am saving money to free myself for more travel.'
Spending money on overpriced food when hungry. The solution: carry snacks. A banana and an apple will cost you, in most places less than a dollar.
Spending on entrance fees to top-rated attractions. If you really want to do it, spend the money happily. If you're conflicted sleep on it. I don't regret spending $200 on a skydive over the Great Barrier Reef, I do regret going to the top of the shard in London for $60. Only you can know but make sure it's your decision and not the marketing directors at said top-rated attraction.
Telling yourself 'you only have the chance to see/eat/experience it now'. While this might be true, make sure YOU WANT to spend the money. Money spent is money you can't invest, and often you can have the same experience for much less.

You can experience luxurious travel on a small budget which will trick your brain into thinking you're already a high-roller, which will mean you'll be more likely to start acting like one and invest your money. Stay in five-star hotels for $5 by booking on the day of your stay on booking.com to enjoy last minute deals. You can go to fancy restaurants using daily deal sites. Ask your airline about last minute upgrades to first-class or business. I paid $100 extra on a $179 ticket to Cuba from Germany to be bumped to Business Class. When you ask you will be surprised what you can get both at hotels and airlines.

Travel, as the saying goes is the only thing you spend money on that makes you richer. In practice, you can easily waste money, making it difficult to enjoy that metaphysical wealth. The biggest money saving secret is to turn bargain hunting into a pleasurable activity, not an annoyance. Budgeting consciously can be fun, don't feel disappointed because you don't spend the $60 to go into an attraction, feel good because soon that $60 will soon be earning money for you. Meaning, you'll have the time and money to enjoy more metaphysical wealth, while your bank balance increases.

PRACTICAL THINGS TO REMEMBER TO SAVE MONEY

- Download google maps for for use offline.
- Download the Paris language pack on google translate - you will be grateful you have it!
- Bring a good mosquito spray or combine a few drops of lemongrass oil with a moisturiser. Mosquitos are a nuance in summertime.
- Know the names of Paris foods to try and the star the restaurants to try them at on Google Maps.
- Don't eat at any restaurants with touts outside. Go away from the main thoroughfare in Paris for cheaper restaurant prices
- Pick up food from the too good to go app - Plan to get your breakfast or dinner from restaurants on the app. $2.99 for a restaurant meal will save you at least $150 on food in Paris.
- Pack food for the airport, you'll save $10 on a bad cup of coffee and stale croissant at the airport.

So there it is, you can save $800 by being strategic with your trip planning. We've arranged everything in the guide to offer the best bang for your buck. Which means we took the view that if it's not a good investment for your money we wouldn't include it. Why would a guide called 'Super Cheap' include lots of overpriced attractions? That said, if you think we've missed something or have unanswered questions just ping me an email philgtang@gmail.com I'm on central Europe time and normally reply within 8 hours of getting your mail.

Don't put your dreams off!

Time is a currency you never get back and travel is its greatest return on investment. Plus now you know you can visit Paris for a fraction of the price most would have you believe.

Thank you for reading

Dear Lovely Reader,

If you have found this book useful, please consider writing a short review on Amazon.

One person from every 1000 readers leaves a review on Amazon. It would mean more than you could ever know if you were one of our 1 in 1000 people to take the time to write a short review.

We are a group of four friends who all met travelling 15 years ago. We believe that great experiences don't need to blow your budget, just your mind.

Thank you so much for reading again and for spending your time and investing your trips future in Super Cheap Guides.

Phil

P.S If you need any more super cheap tips we'd love to hear from you e-mail me at philgtang@gmail.com, we have a lot of contacts in every region, so if there's a specific bargain you're hunting we can help you find it :-)

Thank you for reading

Dear Lovely Reader,

If you have found this book useful, please consider writing a short review on Amazon.

One person from every 1000 readers leaves a review on Amazon. It would mean more than you could ever know if you were one of our 1 in 1000 people to take the time to write a short review.

We are a group of four friends who all met travelling 15 years ago. We believe that great experiences don't need to blow your budget, just your mind.

Thank you so much for reading again and for spending your time and investing your trips future in Super Cheap Insider Guides.

One last note, please don't listen to anyone who says 'Oh no, you can't visit Paris on a budget'. Unlike you they didn't have this book. The truth is you can do ANYWHERE on a budget with the right insider advice and planning. Sure, learning to travel to Paris on a budget that doesn't compromise on anything or drastically compromise on safety or comfort levels is a skill, but this guide has done the detective work for you. Now it is time for you to put the advice into action.

Phil

P.S If you need any more super cheap tips we'd love to hear from you e-mail me at philgtang@gmail.com, we have a lot of contacts in every region, so if there's a specific bargain you're hunting we can help you find it :-)

SHOP 150 VACATIONS UNDER $150.

INCLUDING LONDON.

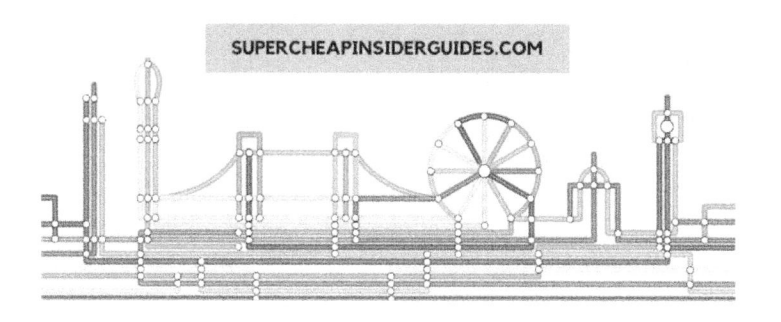

SUPERCHEAPINSIDERGUIDES.COM

UNCOVERED A SUPER CHEAP TIP DURING YOUR TRAVELS? GET PAID FOR IT.
EMAIL PHILGTANG@GMAIL.COM

WE PAY FOR TIPS

CHOOSE FROM PRO RATA ROYALTIES OR A $50 AMAZON VOUCHER

Are you visiting Bordeaux during your France trip? Save more money on your adventure there with Super Cheap Bordeaux.

Bonus Budget Travel Hacks

I've included these bonus travel hacks to help you plan and enjoy your trip to Paris cheaply, joyfully and smoothly. Perhaps they will even inspire you or renew your passion for long-term travel.

From saving space in your pack to scoring cheap flights, there are a wealth of generic travel hacks to help you enjoy stress-free, happier travels without breaking the bank. This is why I've included this bonus section to maximise the value you get from buying this book.

When I tell people I write a travel guide series focused on luxurious budget travel, they wrongly assume that's impossible and often say 'Hitchhiking and couch-surfing?'. Others with more vivid imaginations ask me if I recommend hooking up with older men or women… Of course, they are surprised when I tell them that not one of the 150 Super Cheap Guides endorses such practises because they maximise discomfort. They look at me dumbfounded and ask 'How on earth do you travel comfortably on a budget then?'

Travelling cheaply in a way that doesn't compromise enjoyment, comfort or safety is a skill I have honed over 20 years of travelling. My foremost learning was that locals always know the tricks and tips to enjoy the same or a better tourist experience for a 10th of the cost, and that's why I teamed up with locals in each locale to distil the tips that will save you a fortune without compromising on enjoyment or comfort.

Enjoyable budget travel is about balancing and prioritising what is important to you.
When I tell people about my methodology I often receive long defensive monologues about why they spend so much on travel, or why they can't or don't travel. Thats why we will first discuss how you can find the freedom to travel.

How to find the freedom to travel

Freedom is one of those words that can mean different things to different people. It's important to be clear on what it looks like to you in your life, and all the stories and beliefs that prevent you from having it. For me, freedom means always having at choice in my life. I don't do anything that I don't want to do. —LEO BABAUTA

We've spoken a lot about how to save money travelling to Paris, but how do you find the freedom if you have:

1. Pets
2. Kids
3. A spouse who doesn't want you to travel
4. A job that keeps you at home?

Like everything, there's a solution to every problem. In this chapter, I want to you to think about whether your excuses can be overcome using the following solutions, because as Randy Komisar said: "And then there is the most dangerous risk of all – the risk of spending your life not doing what you want on the bet you can buy yourself the freedom to do it later."

Pets

I have a dog, an extremely loving German Shepherd. And when I travel overland from Austria she comes with me and my wife. If we are heading on a longer trip we either leave her with friends or family or we get someone to house sit for us. housesitters.com offers up people who are vetted and reviewed and in exchange for free accommodation will care for your pets. Just be aware it often works out financially better to rent your space on Airbnb and pay someone to look after your pets. Make sure you visit their facilities before you entrust your pet to anyone and of course, always read the reviews.

I know a lot of people miss their pets travelling which is why we endeavour to take our dog with us. Exploring with her has formed some of our most precious memories. If you're flying with your pet always look up the rules and make sure you comply. If you're going to the UK for example, they quarantine dogs who come in by air. So we only take our dog by car. Coming into the UK by car, dogs must need to be chipped, have a note from a vet saying they are clear of Rabies and tapeworms, have a pet passport and be on a course of medication for tapeworms 2 days before they enter. The UK is the strictest country I've encountered when it comes to travelling with pets so I use this as barometer. My point is, do your homework if you're bringing your furry friend, both about entry conditions and the local environment for your pet. For instance, in India, many domesticated dogs are attacked by street dogs. Educate yourself on your options and limitations but don't think because you have pets that travel is out of the question.

Kids

I also have a daughter who is about to turn 1. We have travelled to seven countries with her so far, with many more in the pipeline. The easiest way to travel with kids is in an RV. You don't have to worry about checking vast amounts of baggage or travelling with a stroller. You have unlimited freedom and can camp for free in many places. You can normally take the RV on a slow ship cheaper than the price of a plane ticket for 3 people.

A [study by Cornell University](#) found that we get more happiness from anticipating a travel experience in comparison to anticipating buying a new possession, so in that way, money can buy you happiness. If you invest in an RV, you can also turn it into a profit centre by renting it out on platforms like www.outdoorsy.com.

You don't necessarily have to fly to travel with kids, train, bus and RV's are better options. Kids become more adaptable and flexible when the world is their classroom. This is true at any age. but when kids immerse themselves in new places and engage with local cultures; this open-mindedness helps them in all aspects of their lives. For school-age children, you are limited to holiday dates, but with 12 weeks off a year, you can still find adventure together.

A spouse who doesn't want you to travel

A loving partner should always want what's best for you. Scientifically, travelling is proven to reduce stress. A study in 2000 study found that men and women who do not take a trip for several years are 30 per cent more likely to have a heart attack. It makes sense because when you travel you are more active; travellers often walk ten miles a day, sightseeing and soaking up new sights and smells.

Travelling also strengthens the 'openness' aspect of your personality and makes you less emotionally reactive to day-to-day changes, improving emotional stability. Sure, losing your baggage or almost missing a connecting flight can be panic-inducing, but, overall, the data supports that travelling is beneficial for you. Tell your partner about these studies, if they don't want a healthier, happier, more emotionally stable you, then it may be time to consider why you're investing your time with this person.

Another common issue is mismatched travel budgets. If you and your partner travel together and they force you to overspend with the 'we're on holiday/vacation!' appendage, here's a tip from one of our writers Kim:

'My husband and I were always having 'discussions' about money during our trips. I love bargains and he is the kind of traveller who's totally cool to be ripped off because he normally travels for business and has become used to spending corporate money. The compromise we reached is that he reads a shoestring or super cheap guide before the trip. Then when he wants to waste money, I say yes, but only in exchange for doing one budget item from the guide. It has worked wonders, lessened our 'discussions' and he now actually chooses cheaper destinations as he sees budgeting as a game.'

A job that keeps you at home

Our lives can feel constantly busy. Sometimes we may feel we are sinking beneath our workload. If you're close to or suffering a burnout the stress relief that comes from novelty and change in the form of new people, sights and experiences is the best remedy you could give to yourself.

If you're in a job that is hurting your health or well-being its time to reconsider why. It is often the case that you believe the work to be deeply rewarding, but if that reward leaves you ill, uninspired and fatigued, you can't help anyone. I learnt this the hard way when I worked for a charity whose mission I deeply resonated with. After 3 years of 70 hour work weeks, I'd lost hair, teeth, direction and, if I'm honest, faith in humanity. It took me 3 years to come back to the light and see that I chose a very stressful job that my body told me repeatedly it could not handle. Travel was a big part of forgiving myself. It helped me put old stories that held me back and probably sent me into this quagmire of self-abuse via work into perspective.

Sometimes we keep letting ourselves make excuses about why we're not travelling because we're scared of the unknown. In such cases, one of three things happens that forces a person from their nest:

- A traumatic event
- Completing a major milestone
- A sudden realisation or epiphany

Do yourself a favour, don't wait for any of those. Decide you want to travel, and book a flight. Our next section takes you through how to book the cheapest possible flight.

HOW TO FIND CHEAP FLIGHTS

"The use of travelling is to regulate imagination by reality, and instead of thinking how things may be, to see them as they are." Samuel Jackson

If you're working full-time you can save yourself a lot of money

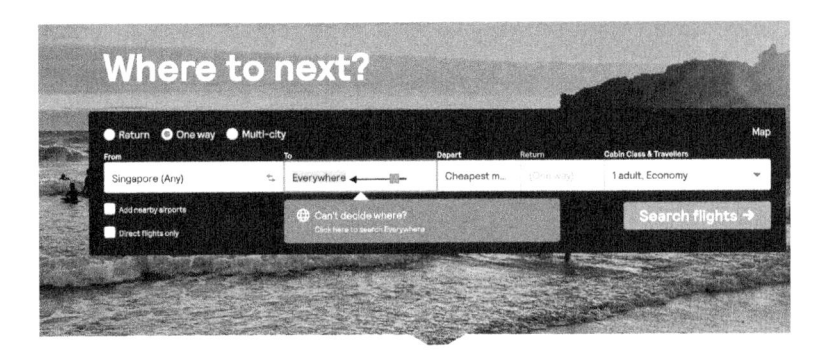

by requesting your time off from work starting in the middle of the week. Tuesdays and Wednesdays are the cheapest days to fly, you can save hundreds just by adjusting your time off.

The simplest secret to booking cheap flights is open parameters. Let's say you want to fly from Chicago to Paris. You need to enter USA to France, you may find flights from NYC to Paris for $70 and can take a cheap flight to NYC. Make sure you calculate full costs, including if you need airport accommodation and of course getting to and from airports, but in every instance open parameters will save you at least half the cost of the flight.

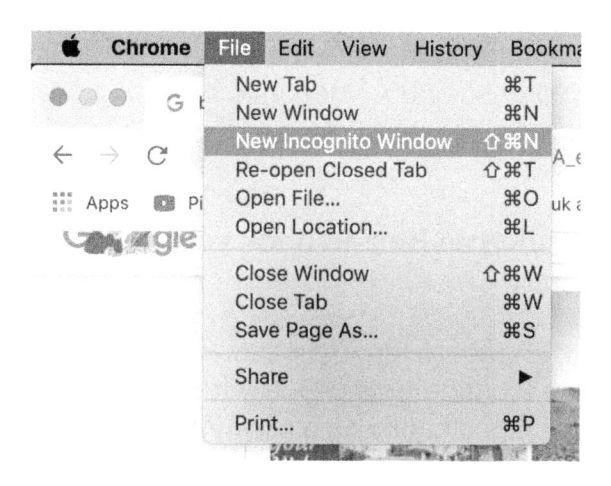

If you're not sure about where you want to go, use open parameters to show you the cheapest destinations from your city.
Use skyscanner.net - they include the low-cost airlines that others like Kayak leave out.

Open parameters can also show you the cheapest dates to fly. If you're flexible you can save up to 80% of the flight cost. Always check the weather at your destination before you book, sometimes a $400 flight will be $20, because its monsoon season. But hey, if you like the rain, why not?

ALWAYS USE A PRIVATE BROWSER TO BOOK FLIGHTS

Skyscanner and other sites track your IP address and put prices up and down based on what they determine your strength of conviction to buy. e.g if you've booked one-way and are looking for the return these sites will jack the prices up by in most cases 50%. Incognito browsing pays.

Use a VPN such as Hola to book your flight from your destination

Install Hola, change your destination to the country you are flying to. The location from which a ticket is booked can affect the price significantly as algorithms take into account local buying power.

Choose the right time to buy your ticket.

Choose the right time to buy your ticket, as purchasing tickets on a Sunday has been proven to be cheaper. If you can only book during the week, try to do it on a Tuesday.

Mistake fares

Email alerts from individual carriers are where you can find the best 'mistake fares". This is where a computer error has resulted in an airline offering the wrong fare. In my experience its best to sign up to individual carriers email lists but if you ARE lazy Secret Flying puts together a daily roster of mistake fares. Visit to see if there's any errors that can benefit you.

Fly late for cheaper prices.

Red-eye flights, the ones that leave later in the day, are typically cheaper and less crowded, so aim to book that flight if possible. You will also get through the airport much quicker at the end of the day, just make sure there's ground transport available for when you land. You don't want to save $50 on the airfare and spend it on a taxi to your accommodation.

Use this APP for same day flights

If you're plans are flexible, use 'Get The Flight Out' ( ) a fare tracker Hopper that shows you same-day deeply discounted flights. This is best for long-haul flights with major carriers. You can often find a British Airways round-trip from JFK Airport to Heathrow for $300. If you booked this in advance you'd pay at least double.

Take an empty water bottle with you

Airport prices on food and drinks are sky-high. It disgusts me to see some airports charging $10 for a bottle of water. ALWAYS take an empty water bottle with you. It's relatively unknown, but most airports have drinking water fountains past the security check. Just type in your airport name to to locate the fountain. Then once you've passed security (because they don't allow you to take 100ml or more of liquids) you can freely refill your bottle with water.

Round-the-World (RTW) Tickets

It is always cheaper to book your flights using a DIY approach. First, you may decide you want to stay longer in one country, and a RTW will charge you a hefty fee for changing your flight. Secondly, it all depends on where and when you travel and as we have discussed, there are many ways to ensure you pay way less than $1,500 for a year of flights. If you're travelling long-haul, the best strategy is to buy a return ticket, say New York to Bangkok and then take cheap flights or transport around Asia and even to Australia and beyond.

Frequent Flyer Memberships

A frequent-flyer program (FFP) is a loyalty program offered by an airline. They are designed to encourage airline customers to fly more to accumulate points (also called miles, kilometres, or segments) which can be redeemed for air travel or other rewards.

You can sign up with any FFP program for free. There are three major airline alliances in the world: Oneworld, SkyTeam and Star Alliance. I am with One World https://www.oneworld.com/members because the points can be accrued and used for most flights.

The best return on your points is to use them for international business or first class flights with lie-flat seats. You would need 3 times more miles compared to an economy flight, but if you paid cash, you'd pay 5 - 10 times more than the cost of the economy flight, so it really pays to use your points only for upgrades. The worst value for your miles is to buy an economy seat or worse, a gift from the airlines gift-shop.

Sign up for a family/household account to pool miles together. If you share a common address you can claim the miles with most airlines. You can use AwardWallet to keep track of your miles. Remember that they only last for 2 years, so use them before they expire.

Pack like a Pro

"He who would travel happily must travel light." – Antoine de St. Exupery 59.

Travel as lightly as you can. We always need less than we think. You will be very grateful that you have a light pack when changing trains, travelling through the airport, catching a bus, walking to your accommodation, or climbing stairs.

Make a list of what you will wear for 7 days and take only those clothes. You can easily wash your things while you're travelling if you stay in an Airbnb with a washing machine or visit a local laundrette. Roll your clothes for maximum space usage and fewer wrinkles. If you feel really nervous about travelling with such few things make sure you have a dressier outfit, a little black dress for women is always valuable, a shirt for men. Then pack shorts, long pair of pants, loose tops and a hoodie to snuggle in. Remind yourself that a lack of clothing options is an opportunity to find bargain new outfits in thrift stores. You can either sell these on eBay after you've worn them or post them home to yourself. You'll feel less stressed, as you don't have to look after or feel weighed down by excess baggage. Here are three things to remember when packing:

- Co-ordinate colours - make sure everything you bring can be worn together.
- Be happy to do laundry - fresh clothes when you're travelling feels very luxurious.
- Take liquid minis no bigger than 60ml. Liquid is heavy and you simply don't need to carry so much at one time.

Checks to Avoid Fees

Always have 6 months validity on your passport

To enter most countries you need 6 months from the day you land. Factor in different time zones around the world if your passport is on the edge. Airport security will stop you from boarding your flight at the airport if your passport has 5 months and 29 days left.

Google Your Flight Number before you leave for the airport

Easily find out where your plane is from anywhere. Confirm the status of your flight before you leave for the airport with flightaware.com. This can save you long unnecessary wait times.

Check-in online

The founder, Ryan O'Leary of budget airline RyanAir famously said: "We think they should pay €60 for [failing to check-in on-line] being so stupid.". Always check-in online, even for international flights. Cheaper international carriers like Scoot will charge you at the airport to check-in.

Checking Bags

Never, ever check a bag if you possibly can avoid it. It is always cheaper to put heavier items on a ship, rather than take them on a flight with you. Find the best prices for shipping at https://www.parcelmonkey.com/delivery-services/shipping-heavy-items

Use a fragile sticker

Put a 'Fragile' sticker on anything you check to ensure that it's handled better as it goes through security. It'll also be one of the first bags released after the flight, getting you out of the airport quicker.

If you do check your bag, photograph it

Take a photo of your bag before you check it. This will speed up the paperwork if it is damaged or lost.

Relaxing at the airport

The best way to relax at the airport is in a lounge where they provide free food, drinks, comfortable chairs, luxurious amenities (many have showers) and if you're lucky a peaceful ambience. If you're there for a longer time look for Airport Cubicles, sleep pods which charge by the hour.

You can use your FFP Card (Frequent Flyer Memberships) to get into select lounges for free. Check your eligibility before you pay.

If you're travelling a lot I'd recommend to Invest in a Priority Pass for the airport.
It includes 850-plus airport lounges around the world. The cost is $99 for the year and $27 per lounge visit or you can pay $399 for the year all inclusive.

If you need a lounge for a one-off day, you can get a Day Pass. Buy it online for a discount, it always works out cheaper than buying at the airport. Use

Lounges are also great if you're travelling with kids, as they're normally free for kids and will definitely cost you less than snacks for your little ones. The rule is that kids should be seen and not heard, so consider this before taking an overly excited child who wants to run around, or you might be asked to leave even after you've paid.

Money: How to make it, spend it and save it while travelling

How to earn money WHILE travelling

"Twenty years from now you will be more disappointed by the things you didn't do than by the ones you did do. So throw off the bowlines. Sail away from the safe harbour." - H. Jackson Brown

Digital nomads receive a lot of hype. Put simply they are "professionals who work online and therefore don't need to tie themselves to one particular office, city, or even country."

The first step in becoming a digital nomad, earning money while travelling is knowing what you can offer. Your market is the whole world. So, what product or service would you like to offer that they would pay for? Take some time to think about this. In German, they say you should do whatever comes easily to your hand. For example, I've always loved finding bargains, it comes very easily for me. Yet I studied Law and Finance at University, which definitely did not come easy. It's no shock that it didn't transpire into a career. And served more as a lesson in not following my ego.

There are thousands of possibilities to generate income while travelling; offering services like tutorial, coaching, writing service pr blogging. Most travellers I meet try their hand at blogging and earning from the advertisements. This is great if you have some savings, but if you need to earn straight away to travel, this should be on the back burner, as it takes time to establish. Still if this comes easily to you, do it!

You want to make good money fast. Ask yourself, what is it that you are good at and how can you deliver maximum value to other people? Here are some ideas if you're totally dumfounded:

1. Teaching English online - you will need a private room for this. Be aware that if you're from the USA and the country you want to work in requires a federal-level background check, it

may take months, so apply early. Opportunities are on: [t.vip-kid.com.cn](t.vip-kid.com.cn), [abc360.com](abc360.com), italki.com, verbalplanet.com and . You can expect to earn $20 an hour.

2. Work in a hostel. Normally you'll get some cash and free accommodation.
3. Fruit picking. I picked Bananas in Tully Australia for $20 an hour. The jobs are menial but can be quite meditative. Look on WWOOF.org for organic farm work.
4. fiverr.com - offer a small service, like making a video template and changing the content for each buyer.
5. Do freelance work online: marketing, finance, writing, App creation, graphic designer, UX or UI designer, SEO optimizer / expert. Create a profile on upwork.com - you need to put in a lot of work to make this successful, but if you have a unique skill like coding, or marketing it can be very lucrative.
6. Make a udemy.com course. Can you offer a course in something people will pay for? e.g. stock trading, knitting or marketing.
7. Use skype to deliver all manner of services: language lessons, therapy, coaching etc. Google for what you could offer. Most specialisms have a platform you can use to find clients and they will take a cut of your earnings/ require a fee.
8. You could work on luxury yachts in the med. Its hard work, but you can save money - DesperateSailors.com
9. Become an Airbnb experience host - but this requires you to know one place and stay there for a time. And you will need a work visa for that country.
10. Work on a cruise ship. This isn't a digital nomad job but it will help you travel and save at the same time.
11. Rent your place out on airbnb while you travel and get a cleaner to manage it. The easiest solution if you own or have a long-term rent contract.

How to spend money

Budget travel hacking begins with a strategy to spend without fees. Your individual strategy depends greatly on the country you legally reside in as to what cards are available. Happily there are some fin-tech solutions which can save you thousands and are widely available globally. I will address those first:

N26
N26 is a 10-year old digital bank. I have been using them for over 6 years. The key advantage is fee-free card transactions abroad. They have a very elegant app, where you can check your timeline for all transactions listed in realtime or manage your in-app security anywhere. The card you receive is a Mastercard so you can use it everywhere. If you lose the card, you don't have to call anyone, just open the app and swipe 'lock card'. It puts your purchases into a graph automatically so you can see what you spend on. You can open an account from abroad entirely online, all you need is your passport and a camera

Revolut
Revolut is a multi-currency account that allows you to hold and exchange 29 currencies and spend fee-free abroad. It's a UK based neobank, but accepts customers from all over the world.

TransferWise debit card
If you're going to be in one place for a long time the The TransferWise debit card is like having your travel money on a card – it lets you spend money at the real exchange rate.

Monzo
Monzo is good if your UK based. They offer a fee-free UK account. Fee-free international money transfers and fee-free spending abroad.

The downside

The cards above are debit cards, meaning you need to have money in those accounts to spend it. This comes with one big downside: safety. Credit card issuers' have "zero liability" meaning you're not liable for unauthorised charges. All of the cards listed above do provide cover for unauthorised charges but times vary greatly in how quickly you'd get your money back if it were stolen.

The best option is to check in your country to see which credit cards are the best for travelling and set up monthly payments to repay the whole amount so you don't pay unnecessary interest. In the USA, Schwab[1] regularly ranks at the top for travel credit cards. Credit cards are always the safer option when abroad simply because you get your money back faster if its stolen and if you're renting cars, most will give you free insurance when you book the car rental using the card, saving you money.

---

[1] Charles Schwab High Yield Checking accounts refund every single ATM fee worldwide, require no minimum balance and have no monthly fee.

Always withdraw money; never exchange.

Money exchanges whether they be on the streets or in the airports will NEVER give you a good exchange rate. Do not bring bundles of cash. Instead withdraw local currency from the ATM as needed and try to use only free ATM's. Many in airports charge you a fee to withdraw cash. Look for bigger ATM's attached to banks to avoid this.

Recap:

- Take cash from local, non-charging ATMs for the best rates.
- Never change at airport exchange desks unless you absolutely have to, then just change just enough to be able get to a bank ATM.
- Bring a spare credit card for emergencies.
- Split cash in various places on your person (pockets, shoes) and in your luggage. Its never sensible to keep your cash or cards all in one place.
- In higher risk areas, use a money belt under your clothes or put $50 in your shoe or bra.

How to save money while travelling

Saving money while travelling sounds like an oxymoron, but it can be done with little to no effort. Einstein is credited as saying, "Compound interest is the eighth wonder of the world." If you saved and invested $100 today, in 20 years it would be $2,000 thanks to the power of compound interest. It makes sense then to save your money, invest and make even more money.

The Acorns app is a simple system for this. It rounds up your credit card purchases and puts the rest into a savings account. So if you pay for a coffee and its $3.01, you'll save 0.99 cents. You won't even notice you're saving by using this app:

Here are some more generic ways you can always save money while travelling:

Device Safety
Having your phone, iPad or laptop stolen is one BIG and annoying way you can lose money traveling. The simple solution is to use apps to track your devices. Some OSes have this feature built-in. Prey will try your smartphones or laptops (preyproject.com).

Book New Airbnb's
When you take a risk on a new Airbnb listing, you save money. Just make sure the hosts profile is at least 3 years old and has reviews.

If you end up in an overcrowded city

The website   is like Airbnb for camping in people's garden and is a great way to save money if you end up in a city during a big event.

Look out for free classes
Lots of hostels offer free classes for guests. If you're planning to stay in a hostel, check out what classes your hostel offers. I have learnt languages, cooking techniques, dance styles, drawing and all manner of things for free by taking advantage of free classes at hostels.

Get a student discount card
If you're studying buy an ISIC card - International Student Identity Card. It is internationally recognised, valid in 133 countries and offers more than 150,000 discounts!

Instal
Maps me is extremely good for travelling without data. It's like offline google maps without the huge download size.

Always buy travel insurance
Don't travel without travel insurance. It is a small cost to pay compared with what could be a huge medical bill.

Travel Apps That'll Make Budget Travel Easier

Travel apps are useful for booking and managing travel logistics. They have one fatal downside, they can track you in the app and keep prices up. If you face this, access the site from an incognito browser tab.

Here are the best apps and what they can do for you:

- Best For flight Fare-Watching: Hopper.
- Best for booking flights: Skyscanner
- Best for timing airport arrivals: FlightAware - check on delays, cancellations and gate changes.
- Best for overcoming a fear of flying: SkyGuru - turbulence forecasts for the route you're flying.
- Best for sharing your location: TripWhistle - text or send your GPS coordinates or location easily.
- Best for splitting expenses among co-travellers: Splittr, Trip Splitter, Venmo or Splitwise.

We have covered the best apps and websites for Paris in the section above called useful websites.

How NOT to be ripped off

"One of the great things about travel is that you find out how many good, kind people there are."
— Edith Wharton

The quote above may seem ill placed in a chapter entitled how not to be ripped off, but I included it to remind you that the vast majority of people do not want to rip you off. In fact, scammers are normally limited to three situations:

1. Around heavily visited attractions - these places are targeted purposively due to sheer footfall. Many criminals believe ripping people off is simply a numbers game.
2. In cities or countries with low-salaries or communist ideologies. If they can't make money in the country, they seek to scam foreigners. If you have travelled to India, Morocco or Cuba you will have observed this phenomenon.
3. When you are stuck and the person helping you knows you have limited options.

Scammers know that most people will avoid confrontation. Don't feel bad about utterly ignoring someone and saying no. Here are six strategies to avoid being ripped off:

1. **Never ever agree to pay as much as you want. Always decide on a price before.**

Whoever you're dealing with is trained to tell you, they are uninterested in money. This is a trap. If you let people do this they will ask for MUCH MORE money at the end, and because you have used there service, you will feel obliged to pay. This is a conman's trick and nothing more.

2. Pack light

You can move faster and easier. If you take heavy luggage you will end up taking taxi's which are comparatively very costly over time.

3. **NEVER use the airport taxi service. Plan to use public transport before you reach the airport.**

4. **Don't buy a sim card from the airport. Buy from the local supermarkets it will cost 50% less.**

5. **Eat at local restaurants serving regional food**
Food defines culture. Exploring all delights available to the palate doesn't need to cost huge sums.

6. **Ask the locals what something should cost,** and try not to pay over that.

7. **If you find yourself with limited options.** e.g. your taxi dumps you on the side of the road because you refuse to pay more (common in India and parts of South America) don't act desperate and negotiate as if you have other options or you will be extorted.

8. **Don't blindly rely on social media**

Let's say you post in a Facebook group that you want tips for travelling to The Maldives. A lot of the comments you will receive come from guides, hosts and restaurants doing their own promotion. It's estimated that 50% or more of Facebook's current monthly active users are fake[2]. And what's worse, a recent study found Social media platforms leave 95% of reported fake accounts up[3]. These accounts are the digital versions of the men who hang around the Grand Palace in Bangkok telling tourists its closed, to divert you to

---

[2]

[3]

shops where they will receive a commission for bringing you.

It can also be the case that genuine comments come from people who have totally different interests, beliefs and yes, budgets to yours. Make your experience your own and don't believe every comment you read.

Bottom line: use caution when accepting recommendations on social media and always fact-check with your own research.

Small tweaks on the road add up to big differences in your bank balance

Take advantage of other hotel's amenities

If you fancy a swim but you're nowhere near the ocean, try the nearest hotel with a pool. As long as you buy a drink, the hotel staff will likely grant you access.

Fill up your mini bar for free.

Fill up your mini bar for free by storing things from the breakfast bar or grocery shop in your mini bar to give you a greater selection of drinks and food without the hefty price tag.

Save yourself some ironing

Use the steam from the shower to get rid of wrinkles in clothing. If something is creased, leave it trapped with the steam in the bathroom overnight for even better results.

See somewhere else for free

Opt for long stopovers, allowing you to experience another city without spending much money.

Wear your heaviest clothes

on the plane to save weight in your pack, allowing you to bring more with you. Big coats can then be used as pillows to make your flight more comfortable.

Don't get lost while you're away.

Find where you want to go using Google Maps, then type 'OK Maps' into the search bar to store this information for offline viewing.

Use car renting services

Share Now or Car2Go allow you to hire a car for 2 hours for $25 in a lot of Europe.

Share Rides

Use sites like blablacar.com to find others who are driving in your direction. It can be 80% cheaper than normal transport. Just check the drivers reviews.

Use free gym passes

Get a free gym day pass by googling the name of a local gym and free day pass.

When asked by people providing you a service where you are from..

If there's no price list for the service you are asking for, when asked where you are from, Say you are from a lesser-known poorer country. I normally say Macedonia, and if they don't know where it is, add it's a poor country. If you say UK, USA, the majority of Europe bar the well-known poorer countries taxi drivers, tour operators etc will match the price to what they think you pay at home.

Set-up a New Uber/ other car hailing app account for discounts

By googling you can find offers with $50 free for new users in most cities for Uber/ Lyft/ Bolt and alike. Just set up a new gmail.com email account to take advantage.

Where and How to Make Friends

"People don't take trips, trips take people." – John Steinbeck

Become popular at the airport

Want to become popular at the airport? Pack a power bar with multiple outlets and just see how many friends you can make. It's amazing how many people forget their chargers, or who packed them in the luggage that they checked in.

Stay in Hostels

First of all, Hostels don't have to be shared dorms, and they cater to a much wider demographic than is assumed. Hostels are a better environment for meeting people than hotels, and more importantly they tended to open up excursion opportunities that further opened up that opportunity.

Or take up a hobby

If hostels are a definite no-no for you; find an interest. Take up a hobby where you will meet people. I've dived for years and the nature of diving is you're always paired up with a dive buddy. I met a lot of interesting people that way.

When unpleasantries come your way...

We all have our good and bad days travelling, and on a bad day you can feel like just taking a flight home. Here are some ways to overcome common travel problems:

Anxiety when flying

It has been over 40 years since a plane has been brought down by turbulence. Repeat that number to yourself: 40 years! Planes are built to withstand lighting strikes, extreme storms and ultimately can adjust course to get out of their way. Landing and take off are when the most accidents happen, but you have statistically three times the chance of winning a huge jackpot lottery, then you do of dying in a plane crash.

If you feel afraid on the flight focus on your breathing saying the word 'smooth' over and over until the flight is smooth. Always check the airline safety record on airlinerating.com I was surprised to learn Ryanair and Easyjet as much less safe than Wizz Air according to those ratings because they sell similarly priced flights. If there is extreme turbulence, I feel much better knowing I'm in a 7 star safety plane.

Wanting to sleep instead of seeing new places

This is a common problem. Just relax, there's little point doing fun things when you feel tired. Factor in jet-lag to your travel plans. When you're rested and alert you'll enjoy your new temporary home much more. Many people hate the first week of a long-trip because of jet-lag and often blame this on their first destination, but its rarely true. Ask travellers who 'hate' a particular place and you will see, that very often they either had jet-lag or an unpleasant journey there.

Going over budget

Come back from a trip to a monster credit card bill? Hopefully this guide has prevented you from returning to an unwanted bill. Of course, there are costs that can creep up and this is a reminder about how to prevent them making their way on to your credit card bill:

- To and from the airport. Solution: leave adequate time and take the cheapest method - book before.
- Baggage. Solution: take hand luggage and post things you might need to yourself.
- Eating out. Solution: go to cheap eats places and suggest those to friends.
- Parking. Solution: use apps to find free parking
- Tipping. Solution Leave a modest tip and tell the server you will write them a nice review.
- Souvenirs. Solution: fridge magnets only.
- Giving to the poor. (This one still gets me, but if you're giving away $10 a day - it adds up) Solution: volunteer your time instead and recognise that in tourist destinations many beggars are run by organised crime gangs.

Price v Comfort

I love traveling, I don't love struggling. I like decent accommodation, being able to eat properly and see places and enjoy. I am never in the mood for low cost airlines or crappy transfers so here's what I do to save money.

- Avoid organised tours unless you are going to a place where safety is a real issue. They are expensive and constrain your wanderlust to typical things. I only recommend them in Algeria, Iran and Papua New Guinea - where language and gender views pose serious problems all cured by a reputable tour organiser.
- Eat what the locals do.
- Cook in your airbnb/ hostel where restaurants are expensive.
- Shop at local markets.
- Spend time choosing your flight, and check the operator on arilineratings.com
- Mix up hostels and Airbnbs. Hostels for meeting people, Airbnb for relaxing and feeling 'at home'.

Not knowing where free toilets are

Use Toilet Finder - https://play.google.com/store/apps/details?id=com.bto.toilet&hl=en

Your airbnb is awful

Airbnb customer service is notoriously bad. Help yourself out. Try to sort things out with the host, but if you can't, take photos of everything e.g bed, bathroom, mess, doors, contact them within 24 hours. Tell them you had to leave and pay for new accommodation. Ask politely for a full refund including booking fees. With photographic evidence and your new accommodation receipt, they can't refuse.

The airline loses your bag

Go to the Luggage desk before leaving the airport and report the bag missing.
Most airlines will give you an overnight bag, ask where your staying and return the bag to you within three days. Its extremely rare for them to completely lose it due to technological innovation, but if that happens you should submit an insurance claim after the

three days is up, including receipts for everything your had to buy in the interim.

Your travel companion lets you down.

Whether it's a breakup or a friend cancelling, it sucks and can ramp up costs. The easiest solution to finding a new travel companion is to go to a well-reviewed hostel and find someone you want to travel with. You should spend at least three days getting to know this person before you suggest travelling together. Finding someone in person is always better than finding someone online, because you can get a better idea of whether you will have a smooth journey together. Travel can make or break friendships.

Culture shock

I had one of the strongest culture shocks while spending 6 months in Japan. It was overwhelming how much I had to prepare when I went outside of the door (googling words and sentences what to use, where to go, which station and train line to use, what is this food called in Japanese and how does its look etc.). I was so tired constantly but in the end I just let go and went with my extremely bad Japanese. If you feel culture shocked its because your brain is referencing your surroundings to what you know. Stop comparing, have Google translate downloaded and relax.

Your Car rental insurance is crazy expensive

I always use carrentals.com and book with a credit card. Most credit cards will give you free insurance for the car, so you don't need to pay the extra.

You're sick

First off ALWAYS, purchase travel insurance. Including emergency transport up to $500k even to back home, which is usually less than $10 additional. I use https://www.comparethemarket.com/travel-insurance/ to find the best days. If I am sick I normally check into a hotel with room service and ride it out.

Make a Medication Travel Kit

Take travel sized medications with you:

- Antidiarrheal medication (for example, bismuth subsalicylate, loperamide)
- Medicine for pain or fever (such as acetaminophen, aspirin, or ibuprofen)
- Throat Lozenges

Save yourself from most travel related hassles

- Do not make jokes with immigration and customs staff. A misunderstanding can lead to HUGE fines.

- Book the most direct flight you can find, nonstop if possible.

- Carry a US$50 bill for emergency cash. I have entered a country and all ATM and credit card systems were down. US$ can be exchanged nearly anywhere in the world and is useful in extreme situations, but where possible don't exchange, as you will lose money.

- Check, and recheck, required visas and such BEFORE the day of your trip. Some countries, for instance, require a ticket out of the country in order to enter. Others, like the

US and Australia, require electronic authorisation in advance.

- Airport security is asinine and inconsistent around the world. Keep this in mind when connecting flights. Always leave at least 2 hours for international connections or international to domestic. In London Stansted for example, they force you to buy one of their plastic bags, and remove your liquids from your own plastic bag…. just to make money from you. And this adds to the time it will take to get through security so lines are long.

- Wiki travel is perfect to use for a lay of the land.

- Expensive luggage rarely lasts longer than cheap luggage, in my experience. Fancy leather bags are toast with air travel.
-

Food

- When it comes to food, eat in local restaurants, not tourist-geared joints. Any place with the menu in three or more languages is going to be overpriced.
- Take a spork - a knife, spoon and fork all in one.

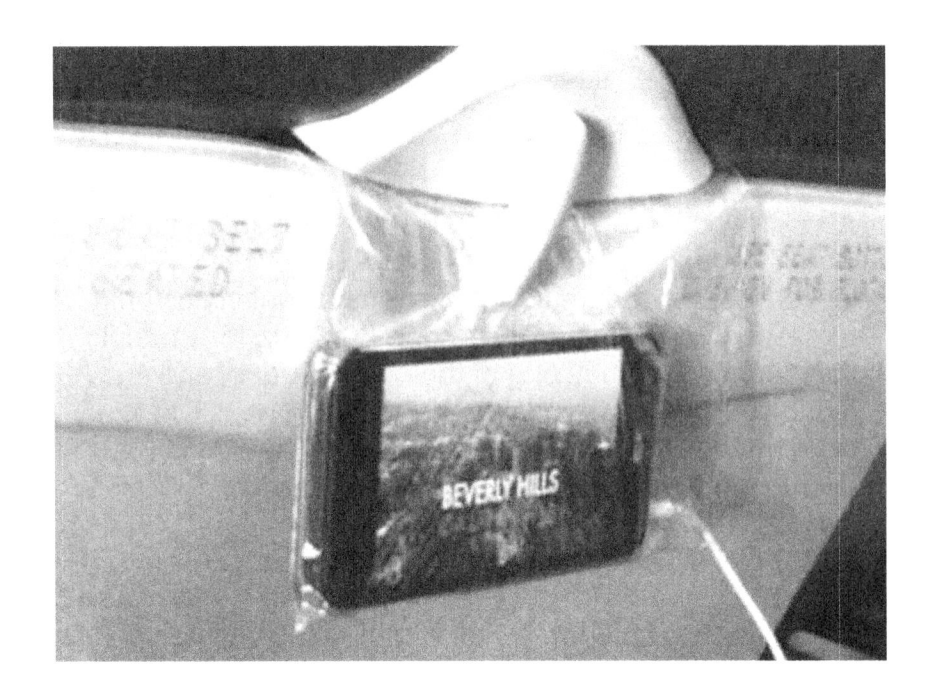

Water Bottle

Take a water bottle with a filter. We love these ones from Water to Go.
Empty it before airport security and separate the bottle and filter as some airport people will try and claim it has liquids…

Bug Sprays

If you're heading somewhere tropical spray your clothes with Permethrin before you travel. It lasts 40 washes and saves space in your bag. A 'Bite Away' zapper can be used after the bite to totally erase it. It cuts down on the itching and erases the bite from your skin.

Order free mini's

Don't buy those expensive travel sized toiletries, order travel sized freebies online. This gives you the opportunity to try brands you've never used before, and who knows, you might even find your new favourite soap.

Take a waterproof bag

If you're travelling alone you can swim without worrying about your phone, wallet and passport laying on the beach. You can also use it as a source of entertainment on those ultra budget flights.

Make a private entertainment centre anywhere

Always take an eye-mask, earplugs, a scarf and a kindle reader - so you can sleep and entertain yourself anywhere!

The best Travel Gadgets

The door alarm

If you're nervous and staying in private rooms or airbnbs take a door alarm. For those times when you just don't feel safe, it can help you fall asleep. You can get tiny ones for less than $10 from Amazon:

Smart Blanket

Amazon sells a 6 in 1 heating blanket that is very useful for cold plane or bus trips. Its great if you have poor circulation as it becomes a detachable Foot Warmer: Amazon http://amzn.to/2hTYlOP I paid $49.00.

The coat that becomes a tent

https://www.adiff.com/products/tent-jacket. This is great if you're going to be doing a lot of camping.

Clever Tank Top with Secret Pockets

Keep your valuables safe in this top. Perfect for all climates.

on Amazon for $39.90

Optical Camera Lens for Smartphones and Tablets
Leave your bulky camera at home. Turn your device into a high-performance camera. Buy on Amazon for $9.95

Travel-sized Wireless Router with USB Media Storage

Convert any wired network to a wireless network. Buy on Amazon for $17.99

Buy a Scrubba Bag to wash your clothes on the go
Or a cheaper imitable. You can wash your clothes on the go.

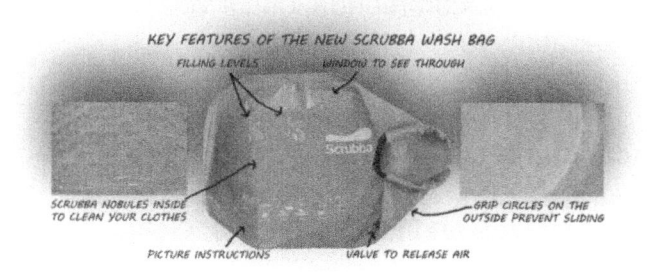

Hacks for Families

Rent an Airbnb apartment so you can cook

Apartments are much better for families, as you have all the amenities you'd have at home. They are normally cheaper per person too. We are the first travel guide publisher to include Airbnb's in our recommendations if you think any of these need updating you can email me at philgtang@gmail.com

Shop at local markets

Eat seasonal products and local products. Get closer to the local market and observe the prices and the offer. What you can find more easily, will be the cheapest

Take Free Tours

Download free podcast tours of the destination you are visiting. The podcast will tell you where to start, where to go, and what to look for. Often you can find multiple podcast tours of the same place. Listen to all of them if you like, each one will tell you a little something new.

Pack Extra Ear Phones

If you go on a museum tour, they often have audio guides. Instead of having to rent one for each person, take some extra earphones. Most audio tour devices have a place to plug in a second set.

Buy Souvenirs Ahead of Time

If you are buying souvenirs someone touristy, you are paying a premium price. By ordering the same exact products online, you can save a lot of money.

Use Cheap Transportation

Do as the locals do, including weekly passes.

Carry Reusable Water Bottles

Spending money on water and other beverages can quickly add up. Instead of paying for drinks, take some refillable water bottles.

Combine Attractions

Many major cities offer ticket bundles where one price gets you into 5 or 6 popular attractions. You will need to plan ahead of time to decide what things you plan to do on vacation and see if they are selling these activities together.

Pack Snacks

Granola bars, apples, baby carrots, bananas, cheese crackers, juice boxes, pretzels, fruit snacks, apple sauce, grapes, and veggie chips.

Stick to Carry-On Bags

Do not pay to check a large bag. Even a small child can pull a carry-on.

Visit free art galleries and museums

Just google the name + free days.

Eat Street Food

There's a lot of unnecessary fear around this. You can watch the food prepared. Go for the stands that have a steady queue.

Travel Gadgets for Families

Dropcam

Are what-if scenarios playing out in your head? Then you need Dropcam.

'Dropcam HD Internet Wi-Fi Video Monitoring Cameras help you watch what you love from anywhere. In less than a minute, you'll have it setup and securely streaming video to you over your home Wi-Fi. Watch what you love while away with Dropcam HD.'

Approximate Price: $139

Kelty-Child-Carrier

Voted as one of the best hiking essentials if you're traveling with kids and can carry a child up to 18kg.

Jetkids Bedbox

No more giving up your own personal space on the plane with this suitcase that becomes a bed.

Safety

"If you think adventure is dangerous, try routine. It's lethal." – Paulo Coelho

Backpacker murdered is a media headline that leads people to think traveling is more dangerous than it is. The media sensationalise the rare murders and deaths of backpackers and travellers. The actual chances of you dying abroad are extremely extremely low.

Let's take the USA as an example. In 2018, 724 Americans **died** from unnatural causes, 167 died from car accidents, while the majority of the other deaths resulted from drownings, suicides, and non-vehicular accidents. Contrast this with the 15,000 murders in the US in 2018, and travelling abroad looks much safer than staying at home.

There are many thing you can to keep yourself save. Here are out tips.

1. Always check fco.co.uk before travelling. NEVER RELY on websites or books. Things are changing constantly and the FCO's (UK's foreign office) advice is always UP TO DATE (hourly) and extremely conservative.
2. Check your mindset. I've travelled alone to over 180 countries and the main thing I learnt is if you walk around scared, or anticipating you're going to be pickpocketed, your constant fear will attract bad energy. Murders or attacks on travellers are the mainstay of media, not reality, especially in countries familiar with travellers. The only place I had cause to genuinely fear for my life was Papa New Guinea - where nothing actually happened to me only my own panic over culture shock.

There are many things you can do to stop yourself being victim to the two main problems when travelling: theft or being scammed.

I will address theft first. Here are my top tips:

- Stay alert while you're out and always have an exit strategy.
- Keep your money in a few different places on your person and your passport somewhere it can't be grabbed.
- Take a photo of your passport on your phone incase. If you do lose it, google for your embassy, you can usually get a temporary pretty fast.
- Google safety tips for traveling in your country to help yourself out and memorise the emergency number.
- At hostels keep your large bag in the room far under the bed/ out of the way with a lock on the zipper.
- On buses/trains I would even lock my bag to the luggage rack.
- Get a personal keychain alarm. The sound will scare anyone away.
- Don't wear any jewellery. A man attempted to rob a friend of her engagement ring in Bogota, Colombia, and in hindsight I wished I'd told her to leave it at home/wear it on a hidden necklace, as the chaos it created was avoidable.
- Don't turn your back to traffic while you use your phone.
- When traveling in the tuktuk sit in the middle and keep your bag secure. Wear sunglasses as dust can easily get in your eyes.
- Don't let anyone give you flowers, bracelets, or any type of trinket, even if they insist it's for free and compliment you like crazy.
- Don't let strangers know that you are alone - unless they are travel friends ;-)
- Lastly, and most importantly -Trust your gut! If it doesn't feel right, it isn't.

Hilarious Travel Stories

I have compiled these short stories from fellow travellers to pick you up when you're feeling down. Life on the road isn't always easy and we've all had those days when we want to stay in bed and forget the world exists. Laughter is the best way I know to shake those feelings. All people who have shared these stories wanted to remain anonymous. After reading them I think you'll understand why…

I mentioned my wife earlier, so its only fair she be the first story. Don't worry she has given me permission to share.

A marriage up the wall

'Delhi belly got me on the third day into the trip to India. I was vomiting so much that I couldn't keep even water down so I went to a health clinic for tourists. Whilst I was there I was asked to poop into a jar and happily put on a drip.

The doctor attending me was mid to late 40's and very creepy. I decided I'd leave the clinic after my 4th bag of fluids because I felt better and was weirded out by the intense stares of my doctor. As I was paying the bill, the doctor came over, dropped to one knee and asked me to marry him at the desk. I stuttered in shock that I was already was married. He was holding a jar of my poo in his hand, stood and then chucked it at the wall. The jar broke open and my watery specimen was literally smeared across the wall as he trudged off. The woman serving me bobbed her head from side to side as if we were discussing the weather and said 'its not personal madam, you look like his last wife.'

Glass shame

'I was in Nashville airport in the smoking room. I heard my name being called for my flight so I rushed out but instead of rushing through the door, I walked smack into the glass. When I opened the door the entire departure lounge was roaring with laughter.'

The Dashing Date

'I had a date with a fellow Brit in Medellin. I went to the bathroom and when I came back, I asked him if he had paid the bill and he replied 'yes'. We were going down some stairs when he suddenly shouted at me to run. Yes, the restaurant staff were running after us because he hadn't paid.'

A fear of farting in hostels

'When I arrived to stay in my first ever hostel in London, I realised I had an intense fear
farting in my sleep. I literally gave myself such bad constipation I had to go to hospital. It turns out an enema is worse than hostel farting.'

What a boob

I fell on the Tube in London getting into a carriage. Unfortunately I managed to grab a woman's boob on the way to the floor. I was so mortified I walked everywhere else during the trip.'

Cementing a few laughs

'I was walking on the streets in Singapore when they were fixing the roads. I somehow stepped in fresh cement. I only noticed when my feet became so heavy I thought I had twisted my ankle. The cement got so hard, I had to take them off as I couldn't pick up my feet. Locals were very clearly entertained as I walked in my sponge bob squarepants socks.

If you've got a hilarious travel story you'd love to share, email me at   . All identifying details will be removed.

How I got hooked on budget travelling

'We're on holiday' is what my dad used to say to justify getting us in so much debt we lost our home and all our things when I was 11. We moved from the suburban bliss of Hemel Hempstead to a run down council estate in inner-city London, near my dad's new job as a refuge collector, a fancy word for dustbin man. I lost all my school friends while watching my dad go through a nervous breakdown.

My dad loved walking up a hotel lobby desk without a care in the world. So much so, that he booked overpriced holidays on credit cards. A lot of holidays. As it turned out we couldn't afford any of them. In the end, my dad had no choice but to declare bankruptcy. When my mum realised he'd racked up so much debt our family unit dissolved. A neat and perhaps as painless a summary of events that lead me to my life's passion: budget travel that doesn't compromise on fun, safety or comfort.

I started travelling full-time at the age of 18. I wrote the first Super Cheap Insider guide for friends visiting Norway - which I did for a month on less than $250. When sales reached 10,000 I decided to form the Super Cheap Insider Guides company. As I know from first-hand experience debt can be a noose around our necks, and saying 'oh come on, we're on vacation' isn't a get out of jail free card.

Before I embarked upon writing Super Cheap Insider guides many, many people told me that my dream was impossible, travelling on a budget could never be comfortable. I hope this guide has proved to you what I have known for a long-time: budget travel can feel luxurious when you know and use the insider hacks.

And apologies, if I depressed you with my tale of woe. My dad is now happily remarried and works as a chef in London at a fancy hotel - the kind he used to take us too!

A final word...

There's a simple system you can use to think about budget travel. In life we can choose two of the following: cheap, fast or quality. So if you want it Cheap and fast you will get a lower quality service. Fast-food is the perfect example. The system holds true for purchasing anything while travelling. I always choose cheap and quality, except in times where I am really limited on time. Normally you can make small tweaks to make this work for you. Ultimately you must make choices about what's most important to you.

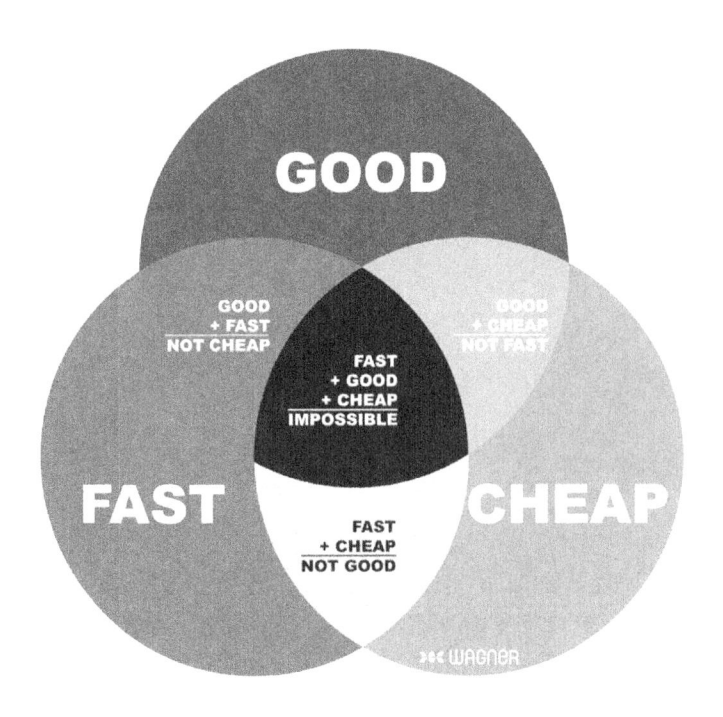

Our Writers

Phil Tang was born in London to Irish immigrant, Phil graduated from The London School of Economics with a degree in Law. Now he travels full-time in search of travel bargains with his wife, dog and 1 year old daughter.

Ali Blythe has been writing about amazing places for 17 years. He loves travel and especially tiny budgets equalling big adventures nearly as much as his family. He recently trekked the Satopanth Glacier trekking through those ways from where no one else would trek. Ali is an adventurer by nature and bargainist by religion.

Michele Whitter writes about languages and travel. What separates her from other travel writers is her will to explain complex topics in a no-nonsense, straightforward way. She doesn't promise the world. But always delivers step-by-step methods you can immediately implement to travel on a budget.

Kim Mortimer, Kim's input on Super Cheap Insider Guides show you how to stretch your money further so you can travel cheaper, smarter, and with more wanderlust. She loves going over land on horses and helps us refine each guide to keep them effective.

Congratulations, you've saved money and done Good!

We donate 10% of all book profits to charity.

This year we are donating to Animal Shelters including one in Paris. The number of abandoned and homeless dogs and cats in Europe is over 100 million - the problem is particularly bad in the eastern and southern parts of Europe. I'm sure you've seen your fair share of abandoned dogs during your travels: its heart wrenching to see man's best friend starving and alone.

'*My dog Gracie was abandoned on the highway in Slovakia. At just ten months old, they tied her to the railings and left her there. Animal Hope picked her up and took care of her and found her a home with us. She is now a healthy, happy girl and loves travelling with us, getting her nose into new smells and soliciting belly rubs from fellow travellers. What breaks my heart is her 'I haven't been abandoned dance'. She is always so happy that we haven't abandoned her when we collect her from outside a supermarket that she dances on her leash for several minutes. Watch her 'I haven't been abandoned dance' dance* . Money could never buy the happiness she has brought my family and me, but donations can help other abandoned animals like her to find loving homes.'

Katherine Huber, a contributor to Super Cheap Vienna.

Donations are made on the 4th January of each year on profits from the previous year. To nominate a charity to receive 10% of the proceeds of sales from our 2020 editions complete the form here: supercheapinsiderguides.com

Gracie

If you've found this book useful, please consider leaving a short review on Amazon. it would mean a lot.

Copyright

Published in Great Britain in 2019 by Super Cheap Insider Guides LTD.

Copyright © 2019 Super Cheap Insider Guides LTD.

The right of Phil G A Tang to be identified as the Author of the Work has been asserted in accordance with the Copyright, Designs and Patents Act 1988.

All rights reserved.

No part of this publication may be reproduced, stored in a retrieval system, or transmitted, in any form or by any means without the prior written permission of the publisher, nor be otherwise circulated in any form of binding or cover other than that in which it is published and without a similar condition being imposed on the subsequent purchaser.

All rights reserved. No part of this publication may be reproduced, distributed, or transmitted in any form or by any means, including photocopying, recording, or other electronic or mechanical methods, without the prior written permission of the publisher, except in the case of brief quotations embodied in critical reviews and certain other non-commercial uses permitted by copyright law.

Our Mission	6
Redefining Super Cheap	10
Discover Paris	14
Some of Paris' Best Bargains	16
Planning your trip	22
Hack your Paris Accommodation	25
The best price performance location in Paris	32
Use our FREE	33
accommodation finder service	33
How to be a green tourist in Paris	35
Saving money on Paris Food	37
SNAPSHOT: How to enjoy a $1,000 trip to Paris for $200	39
Unique bargains I love in Paris	40
How to use this book	42
OUR SUPER CHEAP TIPS	43
Arriving	43
Getting around	45
The Paris Métro	47
Start with this free tour	48
COMBO PASSES	50
Visit these amazing free Museums	52
Queue Free Louvre	54

Climb the Eiffel Tower	55
Visit Versailles on the cheap	56
Disneyland Paris on the cheap	58
Do a river cruise on the cheap	59
Climb to Sacré-Cœur	60
Visit	61
Galeries Lafayette	61
Church Hop	62
Visit Icons	63
Go Thrift shopping	64
Pack a picnic	65
Explore Street art	67
Explore the markets	68
Hunt for rare first editions	69
Moulin Rouge	70
Do Free yoga	71
People watch outside a café	72
Free entertainment	73
Escape the crowds	74
Food and drink tips	75
Nightlife	77
Not super cheap but loved	79

Don't leave Paris without seeing (at least from outside)	80
Enjoy your first Day for under $20	84
Need to Know	87
Cheapest route to Paris from America	88
Mains under 5 euros	89
Avoid these tourist traps or scams	91
Basic Phrases	92
Getting Out	93
RECAP: How to have a $1,000 trip to Paris on a $200 budget	95
Personal Cost Breakdown	97
Thank you for reading	103
Thank you for reading	104
Bonus Budget Travel Hacks	108
How to find the freedom to travel	110
HOW TO FIND CHEAP FLIGHTS	114
Frequent Flyer Memberships	118
Pack like a Pro	119
Checks to Avoid Fees	120
Relaxing at the airport	122
Money: How to make it, spend it and save it while travelling	124
How to earn money WHILE travelling	125

How to spend money	127
How to save money while travelling	130
Travel Apps That'll Make Budget Travel Easier	132
How NOT to be ripped off	133
Small tweaks on the road add up to big differences in your bank balance	136
Where and How to Make Friends	139
When unpleasantries come your way…	140
Your Car rental insurance is crazy expensive	143
The best Travel Gadgets	148
Hacks for Families	150
Safety	153
Hilarious Travel Stories	155
How I got hooked on budget travelling	158
A final word…	160
Our Writers	161
Copyright	165

Where
NEXT?
ZURICH
2020 TRAVEL GUIDE
VENICE
2020 TRAVEL GUIDE
2020 TRAVEL GUIDE
MILAN
2020 TRAVEL GUIDE
MARRAKESH
2020 TRAVEL GUIDE
AUSTIN
2020 TRAVEL GUIDE
CAPPADOCIA
2020 TRAVEL GUIDE
EDINBURGH
2020 TRAVEL GUIDE
ANTARCTICA
2020 TRAVEL GUIDE
SUPERCHEAPINSIDERGUIDES.COM

HOW DID WE DO?

1 DID WE SAVE YOU MONEY?

2 DID YOU LEARN INSIDER INSIGHTS?

3 DID YOU GET A LIST OF THE BEST CHEAP EATS?

4 DID WE HELP YOU PLAN TO SAVE AND ENJOY MORE?

WHAT CAN WE DO BETTER?
EMAIL ME: PHILGTANG@GMAIL.COM

Printed in Great Britain
by Amazon